U.S. History

People Who Helped Make the Republic Great 1620–Present

By
VICTOR HICKEN, Ph.D.

COPYRIGHT © 2006 Mark Twain Media, Inc.

ISBN 1-58037-333-X

Printing No. CD-404036

Mark Twain Media, Inc., Publishers
Distributed by Carson-Dellosa Publishing Company, Inc.

Revised/Previously published as *American Heroes: 1620–1976*

Table of Contents

Table of Contents (cont.)

Introduction

Students can better understand the world today by learning about the people of yesterday and knowing that they were real people, just like you and me. Through the following sketches of the lives of some of these people, the learner identifies with them as real people. There was never any thought of ranking famous Americans. The principle followed is that there be a happy mix of some of the titanic figures of American History and some of the lesser ones. So it is that here appear the names of Benjamin Franklin, Dorothea Dix, Booker T. Washington, David Farragut, Joseph Warren, and dozens of other biographies. These deal briefly and concisely with people who helped make the republic great.

These biographical sketches act as a springboard for student learning. They are simply starting points for student involvement. Time lines are included in each chapter to give students additional information about the subject and time period. This book supports No Child Left Behind (NCLB) and is correlated with the National Standards for History (NSH) and the National Council for Social Studies (NCSS™) curriculum standards. The "Historical Fact" section of each unit may be used to help the student gain depth in factual knowledge. The "Questions for Research" section offers alternatives to the teacher's own choices for supplemental investigations. Some research possibilities are offered; in other instances, it is suggested that the student find some particular historical fact concerning the biography under study. The encyclopedia or the Internet can be used to acquire additional information, as well as the American Heritage Collection and the *Dictionary of American Biography*. If these are not available in the school library, then your local public library likely has them. References for further reading for those who become interested in finding out additional information about a particular famous American are included in the back of the book.

> "There is little that is more important for an American citizen to know than the history and traditions of his country. Without such knowledge, he stands uncertain and defenseless before the world, knowing neither where he has come from nor where he is going. With such knowledge, he is no longer alone but draws a strength far greater than his own from the cumulative experience of the past and a cumulative vision of the future."
>
> — *John F. Kennedy*

Time Line

Take note of the accomplishments and lifespan of the individuals highlighted in these pages. Use this list to help you understand historical sequence and where each of the "famous" Americans "fits" in this time line of historical events. The events listed cover five to twenty-year time spans.

1600   Settlement in Jamestown; Pocahontas marries John Rolfe; the first slaves appear in America.

1620   *Mayflower Compact* ; Boston Latin School is founded; Harvard College is founded; Roger Williams winters with the Narragansetts.

1640   Old Deluder Satan Law; Scots-Irish begin to arrive in numbers; Maryland Act of Religious Toleration

1660   First Indian Bible; Quakers are persecuted in Virginia; French expand settlements into Illinois; postal service is established from Boston to New York; smallpox epidemics occur in the Colonies.

1680   Charleston, South Carolina, is founded; William Penn establishes a government for Pennsylvania; French-Indian raid on Schenectady; Salem Witchcraft Trials are held; William and Mary College is founded.

1700   Yale is founded; the *Boston Newsletter* is the first newspaper; Pennsylvania (Kentucky) rifle developed; "Mother Goose" rhymes appear.

1720   Continued arrivals of many Germans in Pennsylvania; the Great Awakening, led by Jonathan Edwards; Benjamin Franklin writes *Poor Richard's Almanack*.

1740   Benjamin Franklin invents a new stove for "women"; Princeton is founded; Independence Hall is built in Philadelphia; the first general hospital in Philadelphia; King's College (Columbia University) is founded.

1760   Colonial population is now 1,600,000; Charles Mason and Jeremiah Dixon begin a survey; the Treaty of Paris ends the French and Indian War (Seven Years' War), which had partly been fought in the Colonies.

1765   The first medical school in Philadelphia; John Singleton Copley shows his paintings in London; British troops are quartered in Boston.

1770   Boston Massacre; a stagecoach travels from New York to Philadelphia in one and one-half days; Charles Wilson Peale becomes a promising artist and paints the first of his portraits of Washington.

1775   Thomas Paine writes *Common Sense* ; Virginia abolishes the slave trade; Phi Beta Kappa is founded; Declaration of Independence and the War of Revolution take place.

Time Line (cont.)

1780   Noah Webster publishes *The American Spelling Book*; Franklin invents bifocals; Treaty of Paris ends the Revolutionary War.

1785   Georgia establishes the first state university; increased numbers of Scots-Irish begin to arrive, many of whom are well-educated; U.S. Constitution is written; news arrives of the French Revolution.

1790   Population is nearly 4,000,000 (almost one-fourth African-American); Eli Whitney invents the cotton gin, which firms up slavery as an institution; war in Europe—Washington proclaims neutrality; the Genet affair occurs.

1795   Gilbert Stuart launches his career of pictures of George Washington; undeclared naval war with France; the iron plow is invented; Johnny Appleseed spreads goodwill and apples.

1800   The Library of Congress is established; the capital is now at Washington, D.C.; the Louisiana Purchase; the Jeffersonian "Revolution" begins; there is continued trouble with warring powers of Europe.

1805   Noah Webster composes his *Dictionary*; Robert Fulton constructs the *Clermont*; Lewis and Clark Expedition; Zebulon Pike sights his peak; the African slave trade is forbidden.

1810   The first orchestra in the United States is founded in Massachusetts; the National Road is under construction; Benjamin Rush writes *Diseases of the Mind*; War of 1812; "The Star-Spangled Banner" is written by Francis Scott Key; Washington is burned, but Baltimore is saved.

1815   Baltimore is lighted by gas; William Cullen Bryant composes "Thanatopsis"; settlers flock to the Military Tract in Illinois; Territory Unitarianism emerges in New England; financial panic occurs.

1820   *Rip Van Winkle* is written; the Monroe Doctrine is proclaimed; Old Democracy (Democratic Party) begins to split; the first free public library is established in New Hampshire.

1825   John Quincy Adams is now in the White House; the Erie Canal revolutionizes western trade; James Fenimore Cooper writes *The Last of the Mohicans*; John James Audubon publishes his first important book on wildlife.

1830   The Mormon Church is organized; Peter Cooper builds the first steam-driven locomotive, called Tom Thumb, in New York; Cyrus McCormick invents a reaper; Oberlin College is the first co-ed college in America.

1835   George Bancroft writes *History of the United States of America*; Mt. Holyoke is the first women's college; Asa Gray publishes a botany text; Goodyear vulcanizes rubber.

Time Line (cont.)

1840   Horace Mann establishes educational reforms; Dorothea Dix works to improve prisons and insane asylums; Crawford Long uses anesthetic (ether); Ralph Waldo Emerson publishes essays; Samuel F.B. Morse sends the first telegraphic message.

1845   Edgar Allan Poe writes "The Raven"; Joseph Henry, one of America's great scientists, begins a weather bureau; Elias Howe builds a sewing machine; Henry Wadsworth Longfellow writes "Evangeline"; the War with Mexico is fought; gold is discovered in California.

1850   The Compromise of 1850; Herman Melville writes *Moby Dick*; Franklin Pierce is elected president; trouble begins in Kansas; *Uncle Tom's Cabin* is written by Harriet Beecher Stowe.

1855   Walt Whitman, J. Russell Lowell, and Oliver W. Holmes all publish important works; oil is discovered in Pennsylvania; Abe Lincoln campaigns against Stephen Douglas in Illinois; John Brown attacks Harpers Ferry.

1860   Abraham Lincoln wins the presidency; the secession of the South and war begins; Morrill Act is passed; Vicksburg and Gettysburg battles take place; General Tom Thumb visits the White House.

1865   Lincoln is assassinated; the Civil War ends; the formation of the Westinghouse Air Brake Company; first intercollegiate football game is played; the new president, Andrew Johnson, gets into trouble with Congress.

1870   James McNeill Whistler paints a picture of his mother; Saint-Gaudens shows statue "Hiawatha"; the Chautauqua movement begins.

1875   Alexander Graham Bell invents the telephone; Mark Twain publishes *Tom Sawyer*; Thomas Edison invents the phonograph and the light bulb; Frances Willard presides over the Women's Christian Temperance Union; Ulysses S. Grant is in his last years as U.S. President.

1880   Booker T. Washington founds the Tuskegee Institute; Clara Barton founds the American Red Cross; James Garfield is elected president; the American union movement grows.

1885   France gives the United States the Statue of Liberty; Samuel Gompers founds the American Federation of Labor; Jane Addams establishes Hull House in Chicago; Chester Arthur finishes his term as president.

1890   Women's suffrage begins in Wyoming; basketball is invented; Columbian Exposition in Chicago; Henry Ford builds the first car; William Henry Harrison is president.

1895   Mary Baker Eddy founds the First Church of Christ Scientist; the first comic strip is written; John Philip Sousa composes "The Stars and Stripes Forever"; John Dewey begins a school revolution; Hawaii is annexed.

Time Line (cont.)

1900   Yellow fever is diminished by Walter Reed's efforts; William McKinley is assassinated; the first transatlantic radio broadcast occurs; the first successful airplane flight; Teddy Roosevelt catches the nation's fancy.

1905   The San Francisco earthquake; Theodore Roosevelt is elected for a second term; the Model T Ford revolutionizes the auto industry; Robert Peary reaches the North Pole.

1910   Andrew Carnegie gives huge sums of money to philanthropic enterprises; "Muckrakers" and the Progressive Movement are in full swing; William Howard Taft is in the White House—more trusts are broken; Federal Reserve System is established.

1915   Edgar Lee Masters writes the *Spoon River Anthology*; John J. Pershing chases Pancho Villa; Pulitzer Prizes are begun; Woodrow Wilson wins the Nobel Prize; World War I is underway, and the United States enters the war in 1917.

1920   Warren G. Harding is elected in a landslide; slight economic recession; Sinclair Lewis writes *Main Street*; Teapot Dome Scandal; radio is becoming more commonplace.

1925   Calvin Coolidge is in the White House; the first successful "talkie," *The Jazz Singer*; Charles Lindbergh flies the Atlantic; the Holland Tunnel is built.

1930   Herbert Hoover is in the White House, and the Great Depression is underway; *Show Boat* is a big Broadway hit; Amelia Earhart flies the Atlantic; Franklin Roosevelt wins presidency in 1932.

1935   Dust storms in the West; George Gershwin writes *Porgy and Bess*; Will Rogers is killed; the New Deal is at its apex; Carl Sandburg writes *Abraham Lincoln, The War Years*; Hitler begins Germany's expansion.

1940   FDR gives the "Four Freedoms" speech; Japanese attack Pearl Harbor; U.S. geared to war; John Steinbeck is the leading American writer; the first nuclear reaction; Normandy landings occur in 1944.

1945   War with Germany ends; new antibiotics, penicillin and streptomycin, are discovered; Roosevelt dies; Harry S Truman is the new president; Truman confounds polltakers by winning the presidency in 1948; William Faulkner wins the Nobel Prize.

1950   The Korean War begins; George Marshall wins the Nobel Prize; Dwight D. Eisenhower wins the presidency; the Korean War ends.

1955   Russia shocks the world by launching the first satellite; the Salk polio vaccine now virtually eliminates the dread disease; Little Rock civil rights crisis occurs; Alaska and Hawaii are admitted as new states; Nikita Khrushchev visits the United States.

Time Line (cont.)

1960   John F. Kennedy is elected; Kennedy is assassinated in 1963; Lyndon Johnson is now president, and a huge poverty plan is initiated; the first U.S. space flight; the Vietnam War speeds up.

1965   Civil rights and anti-war riots spread; Lyndon Johnson is elected for second term; Martin Luther King, Jr., is assassinated; Vietnam is now taking a heavier toll; Robert Kennedy is assassinated.

1970   Richard M. Nixon is now president; he begins to wind down the war in Vietnam; Governor George Wallace is shot; Watergate, along with the eventual resignation of President Nixon; President Ford now occupies the White House; oil embargo.

1975   The draft ends; troops are finally withdrawn from Vietnam and prisoners are returned; assassination attempts on President Ford; U.S. celebrates Bicentennial; Jimmy Carter elected president; Panama Canal treaties; Iran hostage crisis.

1980   Ronald Reagan elected president; hostages released from Iran; assassination attempt on President Reagan; SALT talks with U.S.S.R.; U.S. troops invade Grenada; Reagan is reelected; AIDS virus is discovered; first space shuttle flight.

1985   President Reagan and Soviet General Secretary Mikhail Gorbachev hold summit meetings; U.S. warplanes bomb Libya; Iran-Contra scandal; George H.W. Bush is elected president; pro-democracy demonstrations in Tiananmen Square in China; U.S. invades Panama; Berlin Wall falls; Exxon Valdez oil disaster in Alaska.

1990   Persian Gulf War; former Soviet countries become independent; Hubble Space Telescope launched; Los Angeles riots after beating of Rodney King; Bill Clinton is elected president; siege at Waco, Texas; Whitewater Scandal; Clinton is reelected.

1995   Oklahoma City bombing; O.J. Simpson murder trial; President Clinton is impeached but not removed from office; the Unabomber is caught; Columbine High School shooting spree; construction of International Space Station is started

2000   Y2K scare proves groundless; mapping of human genome is completed; George W. Bush is elected president; September 11, 2001, terrorist attacks; U.S. troops invade Afghanistan in War on Terror; U.S. troops invade Iraq; President Bush is reelected.

2005   President Bush begins second term; War on Terror continues in Afghanistan and Iraq; democratic elections take place in Afghanistan and Iraq; Ronald Reagan named "The Greatest American"; Hurricane Katrina devastates the Gulf Coast of the United States; gas prices at all-time highs.

Roger Williams
1603–1683

Roger Williams

Roger Williams was born in London to a middle-class family who had obtained some financial success in business. That he did not come from poorer classes is indicated by the fact that he was educated at Cambridge University, where he was a student of the great lawyer, Sir Edward Coke. His years at Cambridge tended to firm up Williams' non-conformist beliefs in regard to the established Anglican faith.

Not too long after the "Pilgrims" landed at Plymouth in New England, Williams sailed for the New World, arriving in Boston in 1631. He refused offers to become the minister in one Boston church, but in 1633, he went to Salem to minister to a congregation in that town. Almost immediately, he began to cause trouble with the authorities—one leading Puritan referred to Williams as "unsettled in judgments." Not only did he champion the Native American cause, but he began to attack the relationship between the local government and the church—what today would be called a "theocracy." Williams argued for tolerance based upon human dignity and pushed for the separation of church and state.

By 1636 (the same year as the founding of Harvard College), Williams had overdrawn on the patience of the Puritan oligarchy. Forced to flee, he spent the winter with the Narragansett tribe. From this tribe, he obtained a land title to what was to be most of Rhode Island. In this area, he set up a colony that was more tolerant and that did allow for a separation of church and state. In 1639, Williams became a Baptist, a creed that advocated adult immersion and denied the power of the state over matters of conscience.

In 1643, Williams returned to England to seek a charter for his new colony. It was during this time that he wrote *The Bloudy Tenent of Persecution for Cause of Conscience*. The sense of this publication was that (1) all governments were the creatures of men and existed upon the consent and welfare of all men, and (2) rulers were only servants of the people and no more entitled to decide the truth in religion than anyone else.

Upon returning to the Colonies, Williams continued to serve the Rhode Island settlements, and from 1654 to 1657, he acted as the president of the settlement association.

The tolerance implicit in the Rhode Island charter brought other dissidents to the colony. Mrs. Anne Hutchinson was one—a determined woman who argued that scholarly insights and "good works" mattered very little in achieving individual salvation. What was important was God's grace, which fell by divine choice upon such individuals as herself. Mrs. Hutchinson founded the town of Portsmouth in Rhode Island. She eventually moved to New York where she died during a Native American raid.

There seemed to be contradictions between some of Williams' contentions and his actual life. When Native Americans in New England under King Philip arose, burned dozens of towns, and killed several hundred settlers, Williams joined with colonial forces as a soldier, even though he was well into his seventies. "King Philip's War," as the conflict was called, resulted in the final elimination of the Native American problem in New England and the death of King Philip himself. Philip's wife and children were sold into slavery.

All in all, Williams made two major contributions to American life—the separation of church and state and religious freedom.

6

Roger Williams (cont.)

TIME LINE

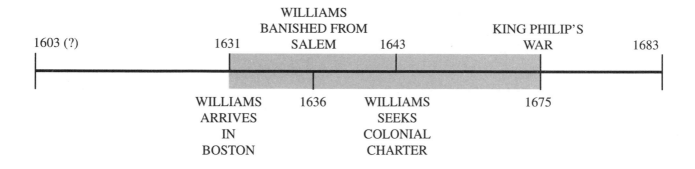

QUESTIONS FOR RESEARCH

1. Shortly after the establishment of Rhode Island as a colony that tolerated other religions, an event occurred in England that decreased the level of tolerance in that country. What was it, and in what ways was there more intolerance?

2. Williams had received an excellent education in England, but he was only one of the colonial leaders having that benefit. Research the education of other colonial leaders. Research the educational levels of the ordinary New England settlers.

3. Shortly after the establishment of Rhode Island, another "toleration" colony was founded. What was it, and just how tolerant was it?

NATIONAL STANDARDS CORRELATIONS

NCSS Ve: (Individuals, Groups, & Institutions) Identify and describe examples of tensions between belief systems and government policies and laws.
NSH Era 2, Standard 2: How political, religious, and social institutions emerged in the English colonies

WEBSITES

http://www.loc.gov/exhibits/religion/re101.html
"America as a Religious Refuge: The Seventeenth Century," The Library of Congress

http://www.yale.edu./lawweb/avalon/states/ri04.htm
"Charter of Rhode Island and Providence Plantations – July 15, 1663," The Avalon Project at Yale Law School

Name: _____ Date: _____

Roger Williams (cont.)

HISTORICAL FACTS

1. Where was Roger Williams born? _____

2. Where did he go to school? _____

3. What was his profession? _____

4. Where and when did he arrive in the New World? _____

5. Did he like the Native Americans? _____

6. What recommendation did Mr. Williams make about church and state? _____

   _____

7. In the winter of 1636, with whom did Williams spend the winter? _____

   _____

8. What did he obtain from them? For what place? _____

9. To what place did Williams return in 1643? _____

   What did he seek? _____

10. What two major contributions did Williams make to American life?

    _____

    _____

11. What other dissident came to the Rhode Island settlements because of the tolerance in its charter?

    _____

12. Williams joined the colonial forces as a soldier in what war with Native Americans?

    _____

Benjamin Franklin

1706–1790

Benjamin Franklin

Benjamin Franklin was one of the great men of his age. Along with George Washington, Thomas Jefferson, and Alexander Hamilton, he was among the leading Americans of the Revolutionary and post-Revolutionary periods.

Franklin was born in Boston, the 15th child in a brood of 17. His father was a chandler; his mother was a strict and authoritarian woman. Although Franklin attended school for a time—long enough to prove himself an undistinguished scholar—he withdrew and went to work for his father. Continuing to be an omnivorous reader, he consumed books on algebra, geometry, navigation, grammar, logic, science, French, German, Italian, Spanish, and Latin.

At 12 years of age, he was apprenticed to his brother James, a printer. Aspiring to write, he produced a series of articles under the pen name of "Mrs. Silence Dogood." James, not knowing that Benjamin had written them, printed the articles in his paper. Eventually, after his identity was discovered, Franklin fled to Philadelphia. Now 17, he worked as a printer and managed to buy a press in 1730. His newspaper, the *Pennsylvania Gazette*, quickly became a success due to its style and wit.

His eventual marriage to Deborah Reed proved to be a happy one only to a degree. Deborah was inclined to nag, simply because she did not understand the extent of Franklin's ambition.

In 1733, he began the publication of *Poor Richard's Almanack*, an annual accomplishment that kept him busy for years. Meanwhile, his fertile mind and unending energy led him into other projects. He was Philadelphia's postmaster for a time and improved on the mail service. He established special messenger services between certain cities. He started the world's first subscription library. He organized a fire department. He reformed the city police and commenced a program to pave and light the streets of the town. He led the fight to establish a hospital in Philadelphia, and he helped to found the American Philosophical Society.

Later, he studied the relationship of electricity to lightning and conducted his famous kite experiments to prove his point. In between times, he studied the flow of ocean currents, invented a new kind of stove, and brought bifocal glasses to the Colonies.

The list of accomplishments in Franklin's life had only begun. He persuaded the British government to drop the Stamp Act. When the Colonies chose the path of independence, he helped write the Declaration of Independence. When the Colonies needed military help, he went to France and persuaded that government to send troops and supplies.

In the Constitutional Convention of 1787, he was the sobering voice of compromise. His last public act was to sign an appeal to Congress calling for the abolition of slavery in America.

He died in April 1790. Approximately 20,000 people attended ceremonies in Philadelphia in his honor. He was buried in Christ Church Cemetery. In anticipation of this event, Franklin had even written his own headstone inscription.

Benjamin Franklin (cont.)

TIME LINE

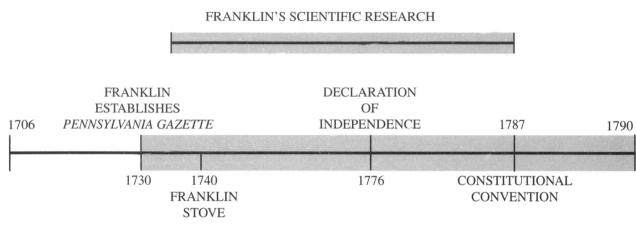

FRANKLIN'S SCIENTIFIC RESEARCH

FRANKLIN
ESTABLISHES
PENNSYLVANIA GAZETTE

DECLARATION
OF
INDEPENDENCE

1706   1787   1790

1730   1740   1776   CONSTITUTIONAL
FRANKLIN   CONVENTION
STOVE

QUESTIONS FOR RESEARCH

1. What were the essential elements for success, as described by Franklin in his *Autobiography?*

2. What were Franklin's major contributions toward the uniting of the Colonies and toward the writing of the Declaration of Independence?

3. Franklin's personal characteristics were in perfect harmony with his goal of obtaining French aid for the American cause. What were these personal characteristics?

NATIONAL STANDARDS CORRELATIONS

NCSS Vf: (Individuals, Groups, & Institutions) Describe the role of institutions in furthering both continuity and change.

NSH Era 3, Standard 1: The causes of the American Revolution, the ideas and interests involved in forging the revolutionary movement, and the reasons for the American victory

WEBSITES

http://www.loc.gov/exhibits/declara/declara1.html
"Declaring Independence: Drafting the Documents," The Library of Congress

http://www.ushistory.org//franklin/index.htm
"The Electric Franklin," Independence Hall Association

http://www.ushistory.org/valleyforge/history/franklin.html
"Franklin's Contributions to the American Revolution as a Diplomat in France," Independence Hall Association

Name: _____ Date: _____

Benjamin Franklin (cont.)

HISTORICAL FACTS

1. Where was Benjamin Franklin born? _____

2. How many brothers and sisters did Franklin have? _____

3. How was he educated? _____

4. At age 12, he became an apprenticed _____.

5. Franklin used the name _____ as his pen name when he wrote a

    series of articles published in his brother's paper.

6. At age 17, Franklin moved to _____.

7. In 1733, he began publication of _____.

8. Name at least three other projects in which Franklin was involved:

    (1) _____

    (2) _____

    (3) _____

9. What was his most famous scientific experiment? _____

    _____

10. What important historical document did he help write? _____

    _____

11. When the Colonies needed military help against the British, where did Franklin seek help?

    _____

12. Franklin's last public act was to sign an appeal to Congress calling for _____

    _____.

James Otis

1725–1783

James Otis was born in West Barnstable, Massachusetts. Little is known of his childhood, except the probability that he was raised by parents steeped in middle-class traditions. He attended Harvard College and graduated in 1743. He soon began to study law and quickly attained success. In 1756, he was chosen as the king's advocate general of the vice-admiralty court. A few years later, he took on the task of acting as the legal representative of the Boston Merchants in their fight against the British Writs of Assistance.

James Otis

These Writs, called by one historian "virtual hunting licenses," gave British officials wide powers in the Colonies. Their usage went back to the first half of the eighteenth century, when it was not uncommon for American merchants to be engaged in smuggling goods past royal port collectors. Prior to 1760, they were not widely enforced, however, and smuggling in and out of the Colonies had become one of the major enterprises of colonial merchants. When King George III ascended the throne, he requested the renewal of the Writs of Assistance in order to cut American trade to the West Indies. Otis was then acting as a counselor to Boston smugglers in their response to the exercise of British power.

The Writs of Assistance allowed authorized customs officers to enter any premises or area during daylight in order to ascertain the possibility of illegal importation or smuggling. Otis argued in the courts that such writs were "instruments of slavery." Otis lost his case, but he did win the public mind with his argumentation.

From that time on, Otis was quite active in the colonial cause. He was one of the four representatives to the General Court from Boston in 1761, and as early as that year, he proposed a meeting of the representatives of all the Colonies. When the Stamp Act was forced upon the colonial governments, Otis reacted by enlarging upon his ideas of unity in the form of the Stamp Act Congress. Due to Otis and other fiery colonial leaders, the Stamp Act was repealed.

Shortly thereafter, however, the British government began to enforce the Townshend Acts upon the Colonies. These were taxes upon various importations to the Colonies, and they represented an attempt by the British government to insert its authority in a broad way into colonial affairs. Once again Otis argued against these "illegalities" and urged the Massachusetts colonial government to lead the way in resisting them. When the British asked Massachusetts to "rescind" its actions of revolt, Otis replied, "We are asked to rescind, are we? Let Great Britain rescind her measures or the Colonies are lost to her forever."

Otis's revolutionary career seemed to be well underway, and with luck he might have assumed a very large role in the events to follow. But fate has a way of toying with the lives of men. In 1769, Otis was attacked by a group of British revenue officers who resented his criticisms of the Empire. The head wound he suffered in the ensuing melee had a lasting effect and was probably the cause of Otis becoming insane. He lingered on past the American Revolution, however—a kind of pathetic monument to free speech and resistance against the British. In 1783, the very year of the treaty ending the Revolutionary War, Otis was struck by lightning and killed.

James Otis (cont.)

TIME LINE

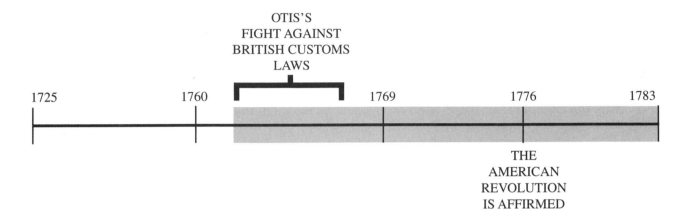

OTIS'S
FIGHT AGAINST
BRITISH CUSTOMS
LAWS

1725   1760   1769   1776   1783

THE
AMERICAN
REVOLUTION
IS AFFIRMED

QUESTIONS FOR RESEARCH

1. When you examine the names of Massachusetts colonials engaged in revolutionary activities in 1775, does it strike you that most were tradesmen or professional men? Why?

2. Was the American Revolution really a war to obtain freedom, or was it a war to keep the British from imposing restrictions on the freedom most Americans already had? Explain.

3. Otis is often credited with saying something to the effect that "taxation without representation is tyranny." Did Americans have any less representation in government than the ordinary Englishman?

NATIONAL STANDARDS CORRELATIONS

NCSS IIf: (Time, Continuity, & Change) Use knowledge of facts and concepts drawn from history, along with methods of historical inquiry, to inform decision-making about and action-taking on public issues.

NSH Era 3, Standard 1: The causes of the American Revolution, the ideas and interests involved in forging the revolutionary movement, and the reasons for the American victory

WEBSITES

http://cdl.library.cornell.edu/cgi-bin/moa/moa-cgi?notisid=ABQ7578-0016-25
"Tudor's Life of James Otis," Cornell University Library

http://www.nhinet.org/ccs/docs/writs.htm
"James Otis: Against Writs of Assistance," National Humanities Institute

Name: _____   Date: _____

James Otis (cont.)

HISTORICAL FACTS

1. Where was James Otis born? _____

2. Where did James attend school? _____

3. What was his profession? _____

4. As legal representative of the Boston merchants, he led them in their fight against the

    _____.

5. These "virtual hunting licenses" allowed _____ to enter

    any premises or area during daylight in order to ascertain the possibility of illegal importation or

    smuggling.

6. Smuggling in and out of the Colonies had become one of the major enterprises of _____

    _____.

7. When the _____ was forced upon the colonial govern-

    ments, Otis reacted by enlarging upon his idea of unity in the form of the Stamp Act Congress.

8. Taxes by the British government on various importations to the Colonies were called the

    _____.

9. Otis urged the _____ to lead the way in resisting them.

10. In a famous quote, Otis replied to the British, "Let Great Britain _____ her

    measures or the Colonies are lost to her forever."

11. In 1769, Otis was attacked by a gang of _____.

12. The head wound he suffered was probably the cause of Otis becoming _____

    _____.

13. In 1783, the very year of the treaty ending the Revolutionary War, Otis was _____

    by _____.

14. His greatest contribution was his fight against _____.

Joseph Warren

1741–1775

Joseph Warren

Joseph Warren was born in Roxbury, Massachusetts, in 1741. He studied at Harvard College in Cambridge and absorbed all that it offered in the way of a classical education. Harvard offered little, if any, science, however, and Warren was interested in the study of medicine. Like others of his time, he learned that profession by performing a kind of apprenticeship in the office of a leading Boston physician. While still in his early twenties, Warren became one of the most respected physicians in the entire Boston area. One may well wonder what his contributions to medicine might have been if the American Revolution had not interceded in his life.

After the enactment of the Stamp Act by the British Parliament, Warren turned to revolutionary activities with great intensity. At the age of twenty-five, he became the leading spokesman in Boston against the restrictive British laws that were being laid upon the Colonies. Warren also served upon various local committees designed to draft protests that were sent to Parliament, as well as published in the Colonies, in order to set forth the colonial arguments.

It was natural that in 1775 he was the choice of the leaders of Boston to serve as president of the Provincial Assembly. His leadership qualities also caused the Provincial Assembly to name him a major general in the Massachusetts colonial militia. It was while exercising this command that Warren became the first prominent casualty of the American Revolution. That unfortunate event occurred at a place called Breed's Hill.

In May 1775, General Gage, commanding the British forces in Boston, obtained reinforcements that brought his total number of men to 6,500. The size of the British force caused Gage—and his subordinate generals, Burgoyne, Clinton, and Howe—to take the position that American rebels should be driven from commanding heights about the harbor.

The colonials under Warren had anticipated such a possibility, however, and on June 16, 1775, the Americans occupied Breed's Hill, which overlooked Boston Harbor from the north. On the following morning, Gage decided to make a frontal attack on the American positions, with the actual field command of the British forces to be placed with General Howe.

The 2,200 Redcoats who formed up to make the attack were ferried from Boston to the Charlestown isthmus, upon which Breed's Hill was located. On a hot June day, the British moved up the hill with heavy packs, and the slowness of their ascent allowed the Americans to hold their fire until it could be most effective. When the British forces were within fifty yards of the American lines, Warren's men opened fire. Twice the British were driven down the hill. During the third attack, the Americans ran out of powder and were forced to flee. But the British suffered over 1,000 casualties during their poorly conducted assault, and in doing so, contributed much to the notion that Americans could fight well against the best-trained British units. It was a notion too quickly grasped by many Americans and would soon prove almost disastrous in other confrontations with British professional soldiers.

One of the devices employed by General Warren at Breed's Hill was the use of sharpshooters. He placed a number of expert riflemen at different points on the hill, each with four or five loaders to provide him with weapons. Their purpose was to shoot down British officers, and they succeeded very well.

Joseph Warren (cont.)

During the attack on Breed's Hill (mistakenly called Bunker Hill), General Warren was killed. His death probably occurred in the third British attack, when Warren was urging the Americans to hold their lines. Warren was exceedingly popular in Boston, and his death was followed by a considerable amount of public mourning.

TIME LINE

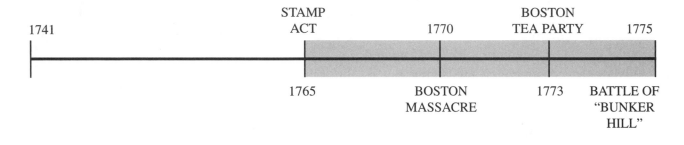

QUESTIONS FOR RESEARCH

1. Why did the British feel that they should occupy the heights about the harbor? List some of the British military units involved in the battle.

2. List some of the character traits obviously possessed by Dr. Warren. Some Bostonians must have described him in some way. Find some of those descriptions.

3. Warren was only thirty-four years of age when he was killed. How old were these men in 1775: Thomas Jefferson, Alexander Hamilton, John and Samuel Adams, and George Washington? Do their ages tell you something?

NATIONAL STANDARDS CORRELATIONS

NCSS IIIc: (People, Places, & Government) Use appropriate resources, data sources, and geographic tools such as aerial photographs, satellite images, geographic information systems (GIS), map projections, and cartography to generate, manipulate, and interpret information such as atlases, databases, grid systems, charts, graphs, and maps.

NSH Era 3, Standard 1: The causes of the American Revolution, the ideas and interests involved in forging the revolutionary movement, and the reasons for the American victory

WEBSITES

http://www.masshist.org/bh/joswarrenbio.html
"'The Decisive Day is Come': The Battle of Bunker Hill," The Massachusetts Historical Society

http://memory.loc.gov/ammem/today/jun17.html
"The Battle of Bunker Hill," The Library of Congress

Name: _____   Date: _____

Joseph Warren (cont.)

HISTORICAL FACTS

1. Joseph Warren was born in _____.

2. He studied at _____, but apprenticed in the office of a

    leading _____.

3. Warren became one of the most respected _____ in the entire Boston

    area.

4. After the enactment of the _____ by the British Parlia-

    ment, Warren turned to revolutionary activities with great intensity.

5. In 1775, he was the choice of the leaders of Boston to serve as _____

    of the _____.

6. He also was named a major general in the _____.

7. It was while exercising this command that Warren became the first prominent casualty

    of the _____.

8. General Warren was killed at _____ overlooking

    _____.

9. When British forces were within _____ yards of the American lines, Warren's

    men opened fire.

10. The British suffered over _____ casualties in the battle of Breed's Hill.

11. One of the devices employed by General Warren at Breed's Hill was the use of _____

    _____.

12. The Battle of Breed's Hill was mistakenly called the Battle of _____.

Ethan Allen

1737–1789

It would not be easy to find a more colorful Revolutionary War figure than Ethan Allen. This unusual man was born in 1737 in Litchfield, Connecticut, the son of Samuel and Mary Baker Allen. Allen's youthful years are a historical blank, for little is known about his education or training. Some historians argue that Allen was about to enter college when his father died in 1755. It is known that Allen fought in the French and Indian War, and by 1769, he had moved to what were called the New Hampshire Grants (now Vermont).

Ethan Allen

Because of a controversy over whether the Grants would be controlled by New York or New Hampshire, Allen helped to organize the "Green Mountain Boys" in 1770. Allen, as the leader of the group, was so troublesome that soon there was a price of twenty pounds for his capture. The reward was increased to one hundred pounds in 1774, which made it quite easy for Allen to join with the other revolutionaries of the time.

In 1775, Allen was elected to write a protest to the King, but the news of the battle of Lexington changed the aims of the Green Mountain organization. Shortly thereafter, Allen received orders to attempt the capture of Fort Ticonderoga. The British troops who occupied this installation were almost totally unprepared for combat. There were too few of them, to begin with, and the officers in command were overcome by a garrison mentality.

On the morning of May 10, 1775, Allen quietly entered the fort, woke the commander, and forced the surrender of the British troops. Although there was little in the way of strategy in the attack, the capture of Fort Ticonderoga was of major importance. The cannons were eventually hauled to Boston, where they were used in the siege of that city. The news of the success at Ticonderoga thrilled every American revolutionary militiaman, so that General Washington's early attempts to raise an army met with initial success.

From 1775 on, however, Allen's fame was rather diminished. Shortly after the capture of Ticonderoga, Allen led a rash attempt to capture Montreal. The result was, instead, the capture of Allen. He was a prisoner of war for over two years, returning to Vermont in 1778 as a result of an exchange for a British colonel.

After his return to the Grants, Allen was made a major general of the Vermont militia. His concept of command at this time seems to have been to engage in a small and ineffectual border war with New York.

In 1780, Allen became engaged in questionable negotiations with the British over the possibility of Vermont becoming either a province of Canada or a possession of Great Britain. Some historians have accused Allen of traitorous conduct, but it is probable that Allen was indulging in a bit of crude diplomacy. Allen wanted Vermont to be recognized by the Continental Congress as a separate state, and by dealing with the British, he so frightened members of that body that he did receive some concessions. Nevertheless, with diminished fame, Allen was forced to return to farming and took no further part in the Revolution.

In 1789, the year of the beginning of the present constitutional government of the United States, Allen died. Some sixty-seven years later, a granite marker was raised over his grave.

Ethan Allen (cont.)

Allen was an unusual man. His publications, which were many, indicate that he was an impulsive and daring man. They show further that he could be vindictive, and that he held some rather radical views about religion.

TIME LINE

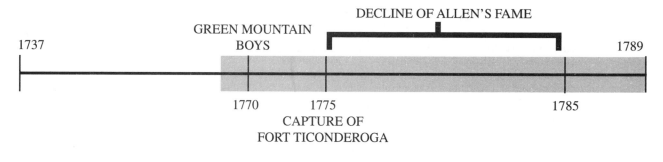

QUESTIONS FOR RESEARCH

1. The Revolutionary War really started in 1775, despite the fact that the Declaration of Independence followed a full year later. Make a list of important events from the beginning of 1775 to July 4, 1776.

2. Look through your library or the Internet, and research the methods and difficulties the rebels had in getting the Ticonderoga cannons to Boston.

3. In what ways was Ethan Allen one of the most rebellious of the rebels? Didn't he even flout the state government by his activities?

NATIONAL STANDARDS CORRELATIONS

NCSS IVc: (Individual Development & Identity) Describe the ways family, gender, ethnicity, nationality, and institutional affiliations contribute to personal identity.
NSH Era 3, Standard 1: The causes of the American Revolution, the ideas and interests involved in forging the revolutionary movement, and the reasons for the American victory

WEBSITES

http://www.ethanallenhomestead.org/history/fort_ti.htm
"What happened at Fort Ticonderoga?," The Ethan Allen Homestead

http://www.americanrevwar.homestead.com/files/ALLEN.htm
"Ethan Allen," The American Revolution Homepage

http://www.historycentral.com/Revolt/battleaccounts/Ticonderoga.html
"Americans Take Ticonderoga," MultiEducator, Inc.

Ethan Allen (cont.)

HISTORICAL FACTS

1. Ethan Allen was born in 1737 in _____.

2. The New Hampshire Grants (now Vermont) were the center of controversy as to whether they would be controlled by _____ or _____.

3. Allen helped to organize the "_____."

4. As leader of this revolutionary group, a reward of _____ was placed on his head by the British in 1774.

5. Allen led his group in the capture of _____ on the morning of May 10, 1775.

6. The cannons captured at this fort were later used by the American revolutionary militiamen at the siege of _____.

7. Allen was captured by the British when he led a rash attempt to capture _____ _____.

8. He was a prisoner of war for over two years, returning to _____ in 1778.

9. After his return to the Grants, Allen was made a major general of the _____ _____.

10. Because Allen engaged in questionable negotiations with the _____, some historians have accused Allen of _____ conduct.

11. Allen was forced to return to _____ and took no further part in the _____.

12. Allen's _____ indicate he was an impulsive and daring man.

Thomas Paine

1737–1809

Thomas Paine

Tom Paine was never really an American, and his contributions to American history were concentrated in but a few years of activity. Yet, he is remembered today as one of the heroes of the American Revolution.

Paine was born in England. His family was so poor that Thomas was forced to go to work at the age of thirteen. At thirty-seven years of age, he was pretty much a failure. It was at this stage of his life that he met Benjamin Franklin. Paine came to America and almost immediately became involved in the colonial propaganda activities that preceded the Revolutionary War. In 1776, when the fighting was already underway, he produced the most brilliant statement of American aims in his pamphlet, *Common Sense*. What Paine said, essentially, is that America had now come too far to return to the British Empire under the old arrangements.

Paine followed this publication with a barrage of other pamphlets and leaflets—the most noted being *The Crisis*. In this are the famous lines: "These are the times that try men's souls. The summer soldier and the sunshine patriot will, in this crisis, shrink from the service of their country..." Almost as much as anything else, Paine's writings held Washington's little army together when affairs were going badly for the Revolutionary cause.

Paine himself served only briefly as a soldier. He continued to occupy minor positions in the newly formed states, and even though he was given rather substantial gifts by Pennsylvania and New York, he was never able to manage his financial affairs properly. He was, in fact, a continuous burden to others.

Paine left for France and later England in 1787. In England, he published a defense of the French Revolution in his *Rights of Man*. Welcomed by the French, Paine worked for the success of the revolution in that country. Once again, however, he managed to antagonize almost everybody and was eventually thrown in jail. While behind bars, he wrote his *Age of Reason*.

Eventually, President Jefferson arranged for Paine's return to the United States; but even at this late stage of his life, Paine continued to quarrel with his benefactors. By this time, Americans in general felt nothing but distaste for Paine's continuous harping upon revolution. Most of all, they were offended by Paine's savage and unwanted attack upon the character of George Washington. It seems that Paine had been offended when Washington failed to act to free him from French jails during his imprisonment.

Paine managed to live past the age of seventy, squandering in his old age various gifts tendered to him by aging participants in the American Revolution. He died in 1809 and was buried in New York. Even after his death, contention followed his name. Ten years following burial, his body was disinterred and removed to England.

For years after Paine's death, Americans continued to regard his historical image with distaste and misgivings. President Theodore Roosevelt once made a cutting remark about Paine. In the 1930s, however, during the New Deal period, Paine was regarded by more liberal historians in a new light. His writings had been powerful and bitter—like his soul—but without them, the Revolution may well have failed.

Thomas Paine (cont.)

TIME LINE

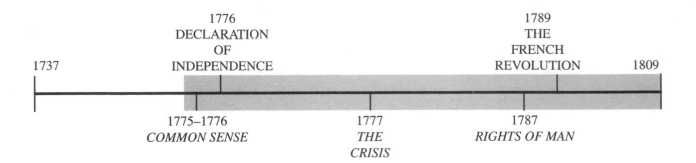

QUESTIONS FOR RESEARCH

1. Why can it properly be said that Thomas Paine was a "professional revolutionary"?

2. Are there evidences of psychological instability in Paine's character? Research his financial and marital situation in Britain at the time of his meeting with Benjamin Franklin.

3. Locate Paine's essays—*Common Sense* and *The Crisis*—and attempt to see why these writings would necessarily exercise a powerful influence upon Americans in 1776 and 1777.

NATIONAL STANDARDS CORRELATIONS

NCSS IIe: (Time, Continuity, & Change) Develop critical sensitivities such as empathy and skepticism regarding attitudes, values, and behaviors of people in different historical contexts
NSH Era 3, Standard 1: The causes of the American Revolution, the ideas and interests involved in forging the revolutionary movement, and the reasons for the American victory

WEBSITES

http://hdl.loc.gov/loc.rbc/rbpe.03902300
"The American Crisis (No. 1) By the author of Common Sense. [Boston] Sold opposite the court house Queen Street [1776]," The Library of Congress

http://www.ushistory.org/paine/
"Thomas Paine," Independence Hall Association

http://odur.let.rug.nl/~usa/B/tpaine/paine.htm
"A Biography of Thomas Paine (1737–1809)," Department of Humanities Computing, University of Groningen, The Netherlands

Name: _____   Date: _____

Thomas Paine (cont.)

HISTORICAL FACTS

1. Was Tom Paine an American? _____

2. Where was he born? _____

3. Was he educated? _____

    At what age did he go to work? _____

4. At age thirty-seven, he met _____.

5. After coming to America, he became involved in the colonial propaganda that preceded

    the _____.

6. In 1776, he produced a brilliant statement of American aims in his pamphlet _____

    _____.

7. This pamphlet said that America had come too far to return to the _____

    _____.

8. Paine's writings held _____ together when affairs were

    going badly for the Revolutionary cause.

9. Paine was never able to manage his financial affairs even though he was given rather substantial

    gifts by _____ and _____.

10. He left for France and then returned to England in 1787, where he published a defense

    of the French Revolution in his "_____."

11. While in jail, he wrote "_____." Eventually, he returned to

    the United States.

12. He died in 1809, was buried in _____, and some years later was

    disinterred and removed to _____.

Francis Marion

1732(?)–1795

Francis Marion

Francis Marion was America's best known guerrilla fighter during the American Revolution. There were other leaders—Thomas Sumter, Andrew Picken, and Elijah Clark —but Marion was the most famous. So elusive was he, that he became known during the Revolution as the "Swamp Fox."

Marion was not a young man when the American Revolution began. He had been a member of the South Carolina Provincial Congress in 1775, and during the rising unrest against the British, he had voted for war. Joining a group of volunteer fighters, he quickly became a captain. During the fight for Charleston, he sprained his ankle and was forced to leave the battlefield early. This was a stroke of good fortune for him, because so many other American officers were captured that he was left as one of the few free American officers to combat the British in South Carolina.

Commanding the American forces in the northern part of South Carolina, Marion was forced to improvise. His men were too few in number to give open battle to the British. Neither were they well enough equipped to face even the smaller British detachments. Marion evolved a series of stratagems that involved surprise attacks and quick withdrawals.

Since Marion's men had to move about the countryside so rapidly, they were instructed to provision themselves. They did away with cumbersome supply wagons. Marion's blacksmiths made swords from saw blades and farm implements. Pewter plates were melted in order to provide lead for bullets. Ammunition was in such short supply that each man was allowed only three rounds per battle.

Marion's hideout was on the Pee Dee River, on an island called Snow Island. The British searched throughout South Carolina, but never came across the guerilla camp. From Snow Island, Marion made quick sorties inside British lines, picking off supplies at one place and driving off horses at another. Occasionally, Marion hit at camps in which the British kept American prisoners, and in doing this, he was able to free many captured rebels.

The British were constantly frustrated. The hated British cavalry officer Banastre Tarleton spent much of his time riding about the countryside in search of the Swamp Fox. Tarleton was a professional soldier; Marion's only previous action had been in a small Indian war in the South.

After the war, Marion went back to a plantation at Pond Bluff in South Carolina. He served continuously in the South Carolina legislature, but the end of the Revolution brought an end to Marion's contributions to the national scene. He did create a legend in his time, however, and one may be sure that Confederate soldiers, almost one hundred years later, remembered that legend well.

Francis Marion (cont.)

TIME LINE

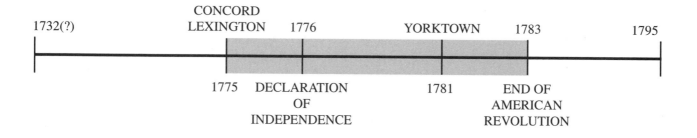

QUESTIONS FOR RESEARCH

1. What geographical factors in South Carolina lent themselves to Marion's type of fighting?

2. In what ways did the guerilla warfare do great damage to the British war effort in the American South during the Revolution?

3. Were there any Confederate leaders in the Civil War who followed Marion's tactics of guerilla warfare?

NATIONAL STANDARDS CORRELATIONS

NCSS IIIi: (People, Places, & Environment) Describe ways that historical events have been influenced by, and have influenced, physical and human geographic factors in local, regional, national, and global settings.

NSH Era 3, Standard 1: The causes of the American Revolution, the ideas and interests involved in forging the revolutionary movement, and the reasons for the American victory

WEBSITES

http://memory.loc.gov/ammem/gmdhtml/armhtml/armhome.html
"The American Revolution and Its Era: Maps and Charts of North America and the West Indies 1750–1789," The Library of Congress

http://memory.loc.gov/learn/features/timeline/amrev/south/south.html
"The American Revolution, 1763–1783," The Library of Congress

http://www.teachersfirst.com/share/states/states.cfm?state=sc
"South Carolina," Network for Instructional TV, Inc.

Francis Marion (cont.)

HISTORICAL FACTS

1. Francis Marion was America's best-known _____ during the American Revolution.

2. There were other leaders—_____, _____, and _____ —but Marion was the most famous.

3. Marion's nickname during the Revolution was _____.

4. He was not a young man when the American Revolution started. In spite of age— _____ years—he was a very successful guerilla fighter.

5. He had been a member of the _____ in 1775, and during the rising unrest against the British, he had voted for war.

6. A _____ was a stroke of good luck for him. When he was forced to leave the battlefield early, thus eluding capture by the British, he was left as one of the few free American officers to combat the British in _____.

7. Marion evolved a series of stratagems that involved _____ and _____.

8. Since Marion's men had to move around the country so rapidly, they were instructed to provision themselves. They did away with cumbersome _____.

9. Pewter plates were melted in order to provide _____ for bullets.

10. Ammunition was in such short supply that each man was allowed only _____ _____.

11. Marion's hideout was the _____, on an island called _____.

12. After the war, Marion went back to a plantation at Pond Bluff in South Carolina. He served continuously in the _____, but the end of the Revolution brought an end to Marion's contributions to the national scene.

John Jay

1745–1829

John Jay

John Jay, born in 1745, was a statesman and a diplomat of the Revolutionary and Federalist periods. He came from French Huguenot stock, one of two famous Americans from that ethnic strain. The other was Paul Revere. Jay was educated by private tutors before he entered King's College in New York, where he developed a fine literary style along with a vanity that both hurt and helped his career.

Jay was admitted to the bar in 1768, and for a while was associated with the influential Robert R. Livingston. When the Revolution came in 1775 and 1776, the Continental Congress had need of diplomats abroad. It sent Arthur Lee and Silas Deane to France, and John Jay to Spain. In Europe Jay did a masterful job, persuading Franklin to engage in secret negotiations in 1782, an act that brought a very favorable treaty for the Americans.

At the end of the Revolution, Spain closed the Mississippi to American trade, an act calculated to cause problems on the frontier. Jay, as the American "secretary of state," tried to solve the situation by conceding some territorial claims in the West. The Congress under the Articles refused to go along with this, however, and for a while, Jay suffered from public rebuke.

After the Constitutional Convention in 1787, Jay, along with Alexander Hamilton and James Madison, campaigned vigorously for public acceptance of the new government. Evidence indicates that all three men wrote essays for *The Federalist*, a pamphlet designed to promote the Constitution. Admittedly, Jay's essays were the least effective of the essays produced by the three. But it must also be added that both Hamilton and Jay were major factors in winning ratification of the Constitution by the New York state legislature.

Possibly as a reward for his work in winning the public over to the new government, Jay was given the post of Chief Justice of the Supreme Court. In that office he was constantly consulted by President Washington, and it was Jay who wrote the first draft of the neutrality proclamation of 1793. Despite the desire of the United States to stay out of the European conflict, the country became subject to various aggressions by France and England. To avoid engagement in the conflict, President Washington sent Jay to London in order to conclude a treaty.

Jay ran into numerous problems. First of all, he had to face American dislike of England, while at the same time his own Federalist government was pro-British. Furthermore, Alexander Hamilton, the extremely pro-British American secretary of the treasury, was guilty of undercutting some of Jay's efforts. Jay's Treaty, as it was called, won few concessions from the British and, in fact, became the subject of public uproar. Jefferson's party leaked details of the treaty to the press and to the public, and some delay occurred in the final acceptance of Jay's work. In the end, however, Jay's Treaty won out, and it did serve to keep the United States out of war for a number of years.

After the defeat of the Federalists in 1800, Jay went back to his 800-acre farm in Westchester County, New York. He lived until 1829, but he spent his last twenty-eight years without real accomplishment.

John Jay (cont.)

Jay lacked the genius of Hamilton and Jefferson, but he was an able man. Despite his famed vanity, he was one of those intellectually vigorous and disciplined men who dominated life in America in the Federalist period.

TIME LINE

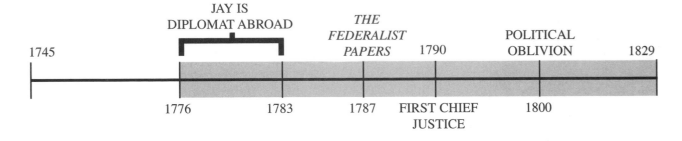

QUESTIONS FOR RESEARCH

1. Jay was considered a conservative during the days prior to the American Revolution. What was he conservative about? Who were some of the other conservatives of that time?

2. Find out why Jay's suggestions to Franklin in 1782 were of prime importance. This may take some digging, but it has to do with a little trick that Franklin played on both the British and the French.

3. What were the terms of the Jay Treaty drawn up during Washington's presidency? Why were the Republicans (Democratic-Republicans) so angry? Which warring powers did the Federalists support? Which did the Republicans?

NATIONAL STANDARDS CORRELATIONS

NCSS IIf: (Time, Continuity, & Change) Use knowledge of facts and concepts drawn from history, along with methods of historical inquiry, to inform decision-making about the action-taking on public issues.
NSH Era 3, Standard 1: The causes of the American Revolution, the ideas and interests involved in forging the revolutionary movement, and the reasons for the American victory

WEBSITES

http://www.yale.edu/lawweb/avalon/diplomacy/britain/jaymenu.htm
"The Jay Treaty of 1794," The Avalon Project at Yale Law School

http://www.columbia.edu/cu/lweb/eresources/archives/jay/biography.html
"A Brief Biography of John Jay," Columbia University

http://bioguide.congress.gov/scropts/biodisplay.pl?index=J000065
"JAY, John, (1745–1829)," Biographical Directory of the United States Congress

Name: _____ Date: _____

John Jay (cont.)

HISTORICAL FACTS

1. John Jay was born in 1745, and was a _____ and a

   _____ of the Revolutionary and Federalist periods.

2. Jay was educated by _____ before he entered

   _____ in New York.

3. He was admitted to the bar in 1768, and for a while was associated with the influential

   _____.

4. The Continental Congress sent Jay to _____ as a diplomat.

5. For a time, John Jay suffered from public rebuke because he conceded to Spain some territorial

   claims in the _____.

6. After the Constitutional Convention in 1787, Jay along with _____ and

   _____, campaigned vigorously for public acceptance of the new gov-

   ernment.

7. Evidence indicates all three men wrote essays for _____, a

   pamphlet designed to promote the Constitution.

8. Both Hamilton and Jay were major factors in winning ratification of the Constitution by the

   _____ state legislature.

9. Jay became Chief Justice of the _____, where he was con-

   stantly consulted by President Washington.

10. Jay wrote the first draft of the _____ proclamation in 1793.

11. Jay's Treaty, as it was called, won few concessions from the British; however, it did keep the

    United States _____ for a number of years.

12. After the defeat of the Federalists in 1800, Jay went back _____

    in Westchester County, New York.

Tecumseh

1768(?)–1813

Tecumseh (Tecumtha) was probably born in what is now Ohio, near what is now called Oldtown. He grew up hating the "long knives," as the Native Americans called the European settlers, who were then moving into the old Northwest Territory. Tecumseh had sufficient reason to hate the Americans, for his father and two of his brothers were killed in battles with American soldiers. In 1800, when Ohio and Indiana saw the arrival of white colonists, Tecumseh decided to fight. He traveled constantly in his efforts to unite Native American tribes in the region, for it was his idea that the Americans exploited and used the enmities that existed between various tribes. He himself was a Shawnee.

Tecumseh

Tecumseh met with considerable success in his drive towards unity. His twin brother, Tenskwatawa, called the "Shawnee Prophet," greatly aided Tecumseh in his efforts. The name "Prophet," so often given to later settlements in the West (Prophetstown), was given to Tenskwatawa because he had once overheard British officers discussing the fact that an eclipse of the sun was due on a certain date. He returned to his tribe and told his people that, at a certain time, the sun would die and then later return. It did, and thereafter he was known as the Prophet.

Tecumseh and the Prophet were fortunate in that they received considerable aid in the form of guns and supplies from the British in Canada. Still, it was Tecumseh's oratorical abilities that made it possible for him to bring about the unity of Native Americans in the Northwest. Some tribes south of the Ohio River were even persuaded to join in Tecumseh's cause.

In 1811, Tecumseh denounced a treaty that William Henry Harrison, a frontier general and governor, had made with the Native Americans. The native chief then went on the warpath, and a number of Americans were killed on the frontier before Tecumseh's forces were attacked by Harrison at Tippecanoe Creek in Indiana. The Native Americans under the Prophet (Tecumseh was elsewhere) fought well, and almost managed a victory. In the end, however, Harrison prevailed, and the American general destroyed the Native American village and various supplies.

During the War of 1812, Tecumseh served as a brigadier general with the British. He continued to hope that the American advance into the Northwest would be halted. In 1813, Harrison got his troops across Lake Erie and fought both Native Americans and British on the Thames River. In this affair, the Battle of the Thames, Tecumseh was killed—reputedly by an American officer named Richard Johnson. Harrison used the fame of his victories to move eventually into the White House; Johnson used his own wartime reputation to vault into the vice-presidency.

Tecumseh was the most able of the Native American chiefs in the time between Pontiac and Chief Joseph of the Nez Percés.

Tecumseh (cont.)

TIME LINE

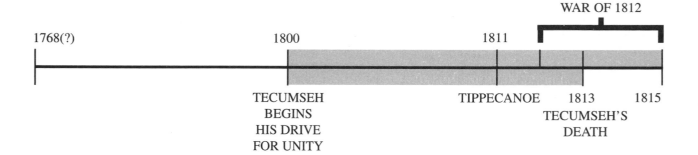

QUESTIONS FOR RESEARCH

1. Why did settlers begin to pour into the Northwest Territory after 1800? Did it have anything to do with land sales?

2. Research the actual fight between Richard Johnson and Tecumseh. How much truth do you think exists in the stories of the battle?

3. What was the relationship between Tecumseh and the War of 1812? Check the votes in the Congress *for* war. From where did they come?

NATIONAL STANDARDS CORRELATIONS

NCSS IId: (Time, Continuity, & Change) Identify and use processes important to reconstructing and reinterpreting the past, such as using a variety of sources, providing, validating, and weighing evidence for claims, checking credibility of sources, and searching for causality.
NSH Era 4, Standard 1: United States territorial expansion between 1801 and 1861, and how it affected relations with external powers and Native Americans

WEBSITES

http://www.ohiohistorycentral.org/ohc/h/peo/tecumseh.shtml
"Tecumseh," Ohio Historical Society

http://usinfo.state.gov/usa/infousa/facts/democrac/5.htm
"The Northwest Ordinance (1787)," U.S. Department of State

http://www.ourdocuments.gov/doc.php?flash=true&doc=8
"Northwest Ordinance (1787)," The U.S. Archives and Records Administration

Name: _____   Date: _____

Tecumseh (cont.)

HISTORICAL FACTS

1. Tecumseh (Tecumtha) was probably born near what is now called Oldtown, in the year _____.

2. The European settlers moving into the old Northwest Territory were called by the Native Americans "_____."

3. Tecumseh hated the Americans for many reasons, among them was the killing of his _____ and _____.

4. This Native American leader was a Shawnee but met with considerable success in his drive for _____ among several tribes.

5. Tecumseh's twin brother, _____, called the "_____," greatly aided him in his efforts.

6. The brother attained his nickname after overhearing the British predicting an _____ of the _____ and then prophesying it to the Shawnees.

7. Tecumseh and his brother were fortunate in that they received considerable aid in the form of guns and supplies from the _____ in Canada.

8. It was Tecumseh's _____ abilities that made it possible to bring about the unity of Native Americans in the Northwest.

9. In 1811, Tecumseh denounced a treaty that _____, a frontier general and governor, had made with the Native Americans.

10. Tecumseh's forces, under the command of his brother "_____," were attacked and defeated by Harrison at _____ .

11. During the War of 1812, Tecumseh served as a _____ with the _____ .

12. In 1813, in the Battle of the Thames, Tecumseh was killed—reputedly by an American officer named _____ who later became Vice President of the United States.

Zebulon Pike

1779–1812

Zebulon Pike

Zebulon Pike was one of America's first genuine heroes. What he did, the manner in which he spent his life, and the way he died caused avid young readers of the United States to enshrine him in their memories. After all, Pike was much closer to the youth of America in age, time, and place than all of the heroes of the American Revolution.

Zebulon Pike had inauspicious beginnings. He was born in New Jersey to a family that could have possibly been classified as middle-class. He had the nominal schooling of the time, which he terminated himself by entering the American army at the age of fifteen. Slowly but surely, he moved up through the ranks. In such a small army as the United States had in the 1790s, it was possible to become well-known for one's versatility. When President Thomas Jefferson, through a combination of happy circumstances, managed the purchase of the Louisiana Territory, he was in need of realizing the exact extent of America's greatest real estate transaction. There were no maps of the Louisiana Territory, and President Jefferson needed answers to some questions.

This is the point at which Pike came to the fore. Mentioned to Jefferson as a capable leader, he was picked by the president to lead an expedition to find the headwaters of the Mississippi River. With a small complement of men, Pike struggled up the great river, mapped the area, and returned to indicate to Jefferson just where those headwaters were. Some years later, other explorations were to prove Pike's calculations wrong—but Jefferson was not to know that. He quickly gave Pike another assignment—to explore the Southwest.

The exact details of Pike's orders were secret. The notorious General James Wilkinson, general-in-chief of the army, interpreted those orders to mean that Pike was to go along the Arkansas River as far as he could. Presumably this meant that Pike was to go west until he ran into the Spanish.

Pike left from St. Louis in 1806, moving westward to Fort Osage and then along the Osage River. He then abruptly veered to the south until he ran into the western reaches of the Arkansas River. When he reached the site of what is now Pueblo, Colorado, he could see the distant peak that was eventually named for him.

At this point, Pike did something most peculiar. He confided to his men that he wished to find the headwaters of the Red River, which was far to the east. Pike crossed the Sangre de Cristo Range where he ran into Spanish troops and was captured. He was taken first to Santa Fe and then eventually farther south. Wherever the Spanish took him, Pike made notes. He kept a kind of diary on geographical features—an action that the Spanish must have allowed him to carry out.

After an imprisonment of a few months, Pike's men were divided into two groups. For some reason, the Spanish sent them back to St. Louis by two separate routes. One of the groups finally reached that town by moving along the El Camino Real. The second detachment disappeared completely. Pike made it back to safety, and his notes proved to be the most important source of information about northern Mexico at the time of the Mexican War.

By the time of the War of 1812, Pike had reached the rank of general. He led an advance against York (now Toronto) in Canada, and during this campaign, lost his life. Legend has it that he was accorded the finest burial possible at the time—that of being interred in a large cask of wine.

Zebulon Pike (cont.)

TIME LINE

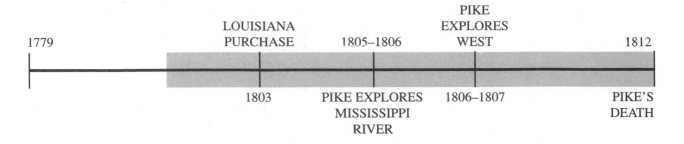

QUESTIONS FOR RESEARCH

1. Locate historical material dealing with the Louisiana Purchase. How was it the result of a happy combination of circumstances?

2. Who was General Wilkinson, and why does he have a bad historical reputation? As a hint, look into the Burr Conspiracy.

3. There were, besides the Pike expeditions, other attempts by Jefferson to explore the Louisiana Territory. Which was the most famous of these, and what were some of the difficulties experienced by the men involved?

NATIONAL STANDARDS CORRELATIONS

NCSS IId: (Time, Continuity, & Change) Identify and use processes important to reconstructing and reinterpreting the past, such as using a variety of sources, providing, validating, and weighing evidence for claims, checking credibility of sources, and searching for causality.

NSH Era 4, Standard 1: United States territorial expansion between 1801 and 1861, and how it affected relations with external powers and Native Americans

WEBSITES

http://www.ourdocuments.gov/doc.php?doc=18
"Louisiana Purchase Treaty (1803)," The U.S. Archives and Records Administration

http://ourdocuments.gov/doc.php?doc=17&page=transcript
"Transcript of Jefferson's Secret Message to Congress Regarding the Lewis & Clark Expedition (1803)," The Library of Congress

http://www.loc.gov/exhibits/lewisandclark/lewis-after.html
"After Lewis and Clark," The Library of Congress

Name: _____   Date: _____

Zebulon Pike (cont.)

HISTORICAL FACTS

1. Zebulon Pike was one of America's first genuine heroes, dying at the young age of _____.

2. Pike was born in New Jersey. The son of a middle-class family, he entered the army at age _____.

3. _____ was president at this time, and through a combination

    of happy circumstances purchased _____.

4. Mentioned to the president as a capable leader, Pike was picked by the president to lead an expe-

    dition to find the headwaters of the _____.

5. After completing what he thought was a successful mapping of the great river, he re-

    ported to the president and was immediately given another assignment—to explore the

    _____.

6. Pike left from St. Louis in 1806, moving westward to Fort Osage and then along the

    _____ River. He then veered south to the _____ River.

7. He then reached the site of what is now Pueblo, Colorado. He could see a distant peak, which

    was eventually named _____ Peak.

8. Pike crossed the Sangre de Cristo Range where he was captured by _____

    troops. He kept a diary on geographical features as he went.

9. His captors divided his men into two groups, sending them back to _____ by

    two separate routes.

10. Pike made it back safely, and his notes proved to be the most important source of information

    about _____ at the time of the _____.

11. By the time of the War of _____, Pike had reached the rank of _____

    _____.

12. He led an advance against _____ (now Toronto) in Canada, and was

    _____.

Black Hawk

1767(?)–1838

Black Hawk

Along the Rock River in Illinois, there is a magnificent statue that dominates the entire valley. Lorado Taft, its sculptor, probably meant it to be a dedicatory symbol to the Native American. Time and custom have now caused it to be called the "Black Hawk" statue.

The Sauk chief Black Hawk was born in a Native American village only two miles above the mouth of the Rock River. One can only estimate the date of the event as 1767, for the natives kept no birth records. His childhood was spent learning traditional lore and crafts and becoming accustomed to dealing with the French and Spanish fur traders of the time.

In 1804, William Henry Harrison, an American frontier fighter, negotiated a treaty with various Sauk and Fox chiefs, in which the Native Americans ceded their rights to the country along the Rock River. Black Hawk, a rising minor chief, refused to recognize this treaty, claiming that the chiefs had signed the agreement while under the influence of liquor. His argument had considerable historical backing, and it is true that Harrison was guilty of treating Native Americans in this fashion in prior treaty arrangements.

But there was more to Black Hawk's distrust of Americans than the Harrison treaty. He recognized the "long knives," as Americans were called, as a much more dangerous threat to Native American life than either the French or the Spanish. Therefore, when the United States went to war against the British in 1812, Black Hawk quickly threw his support to the pro-British chief, Tecumseh.

After the end of the War of 1812, British attempts to conspire with the Native Americans began to decline, and Black Hawk and other chiefs were virtually on their own in their fight against the Americans. Black Hawk made various attempts to form Native American alliances—particularly with the Winnebagoes–all without a great degree of success.

After the War of 1812, the United States gave to the veterans of the recent conflict the bulk of the lands between the Illinois and Mississippi Rivers. When the American frontiersmen began to take up their claims, they were faced with a determined Black Hawk. While others of his tribe had gone with another chief, Keokuk, to lands in Iowa, Black Hawk clung to the ancestral burial ground along the Rock River.

The Black Hawk War, as it became known, wasn't much of a war, although such prominent men as Zachary Taylor, Abraham Lincoln, and Jefferson Davis were involved in it. Eventually, after some very minor successes, Black Hawk fled to Wisconsin with his warriors and their families. There, along the Bad Axe River, American forces caught them and not only captured Black Hawk, but massacred some of the defenseless Native Americans.

Yet Black Hawk was given a kind of special treatment, being taken East where he met President Jackson and other dignitaries. After a brief time in prison in Virginia, Black Hawk was returned to Iowa to the supervision of Chief Keokuk. From this point on, he was no longer anti-American and spent his remaining days dictating his life story to an American army interpreter. Black Hawk died in 1838. His grave was later desecrated, and the bones were lost in a museum fire in Burlington, Iowa.

Black Hawk was a man with fire in his heart and poetry in his soul. His "autobiography" is an American classic.

Black Hawk (cont.)

TIME LINE

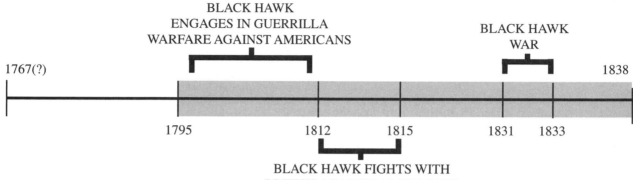

QUESTIONS FOR RESEARCH

1. Black Hawk is usually considered one of the more famous Native American chiefs. How would you rate him alongside other such leaders as Sequoyah, Chief Joseph, or Tecumseh?

2. Abraham Lincoln "fought" in the Black Hawk War. Examine works by Carl Sandburg or Benjamin Thomas as to the kind of adventures experienced by the young "railsplitter."

3. A major figure in the defeat of Native Americans east of the Mississippi was William Henry Harrison. Research his life and his relationships with Native Americans.

NATIONAL STANDARDS CORRELATIONS

NCSS IVf: (Individual Development & Identity) Identify and describe the influence of perception, attitudes, values, and beliefs on personal identity.
NSH Era 4, Standard 1: United States territorial expansion between 1801 and 1861, and how it affected relations with external powers and Native Americans

WEBSITES

http://www.whitehouse.gov/history/presidents/al16.html
"Abraham Lincoln," The White House

http://www.whitehouse.gov/history/presidents/wh9.html
"William Henry Harrison," The White House

http://lincoln.lib.niu.edu/blackhawk/
"The Black Hawk War of 1832," Abraham Lincoln Historical Digitization Project

http://www.americanpresident.org/history/williamhharrison/
"William Henry Harrison (1841)," Miller Center of Public Affairs, University of Virginia

Black Hawk (cont.)

HISTORICAL FACTS

1. The "Black Hawk" statue, along the Rock River in Illinois, was sculpted by _____

   _____.

2. The Sauk chief _____ was born in a Native American

   village only two miles from the mouth of the _____.

3. This Native American's childhood was spent dealing with the _____ and

   _____ fur traders.

4. What American frontier fighter negotiated a treaty with various Sauk and Fox chiefs?

   _____

5. Black Hawk refused to recognize these _____.

6. He recognized the "_____," as the Americans were called, as a

   much more dangerous threat to Native American life than either the French or Spanish.

7. When the United States went to war against the British in 1812, Black Hawk quickly supported

   the pro-British Indian chief, _____.

8. After the War of 1812, the Native Americans were on their own in their fight against the

   _____.

9. Veterans of the War of 1812 were given the bulk of the lands between the _____

   and _____ Rivers.

10. Black Hawk resisted the _____ of these lands.

11. A war was fought for these lands, involving Zachary Taylor, Abraham Lincoln, and Jefferson

    Davis. _____ lost and fled to Wisconsin with his warriors.

12 Black Hawk eventually was taken east where he met President _____. He

    was eventually returned to Iowa to the supervision of _____.

Dolley Madison

1768–1849

Dolley Madison

Dolley Madison was born in Guilford County, North Carolina. Throughout her life, she spelled her first name in the manner of her times, yet it is doubtful that Dolley was really her first name. She was probably given the name Dorothy at birth. Nevertheless, raised as Dolley, she spent part of her childhood in Scotchtown, Virginia. In 1783, the date of the ending of the American Revolution, she and her family moved to Philadelphia. Several years later, in 1790, she married John Todd, Jr., who was a Quaker lawyer. By this marriage she bore two sons. In 1793, both her husband and one of her sons died. A year later, in 1794, she married James Madison who, at the time of the marriage, was a congressman from Virginia.

Dolley's new husband was a remarkable man. He had attended Princeton College as a youth and graduated from that institution in 1771. Throughout the Revolutionary period, James Madison played an important role, although he was generally overshadowed by Thomas Jefferson. In the Constitutional Convention of 1787, he came into his own, however. Jefferson was not present during the sessions, and along with Alexander Hamilton, Madison helped to guide the course of the Convention. When the document was finished, both Madison and Hamilton wrote *The Federalist Papers* in order to persuade a nationwide acceptance of the Constitution.

Four years after Madison's marriage to Dolley, both the Virginia statesman and his wife became disillusioned by the trend of national events. They retired to Madison's estate, apparently intending to live out their lives directing the affairs of that establishment. In 1801, however, President Jefferson appointed Madison to the office of secretary of state, and from that position "little Jimmie" vaulted into the presidency.

Madison's first term was a hectic time in which, on several occasions, war was narrowly averted by the young nation. Finally, in 1812, through a combination of events, Congress voted for, and Madison signed, a declaration of war against Great Britain.

During these presidential years, Dolley tried to bring some life and gaiety to the new city of Washington. During the war, the British landed in Chesapeake Bay, beat some hastily gathered American forces at Blandensburg, and then marched to the capital. The British soldiery burned most of the city; it has been said that when the invaders entered the president's house, they found a still-warm meal that had been hastily left by the president and his wife.

Dolley apparently was the last person to leave the president's house prior to the British entry into Washington. She managed to save a famous painting of President Washington by cutting it from its frame, and she also saved a number of very valuable presidential papers.

Eventually the British marched off, and the President's entourage was able to return to the capital. Dolley quickly reinstituted her elaborate round of social affairs, although she and her husband were not able to live in the blackened presidential mansion. It would be some time before an American president could occupy the president's house.

Dolley Madison (cont.)

We know a good deal about how Dolley Madison looked and dressed. In her middle years, especially, she appears as a sturdy-looking woman who indulged in elaborate coiffures. We also know that she was intelligent in her conversation and innovative in her entertaining. She was the first, First Lady to serve ice cream.

James Madison died in Montpelier, Virginia, in 1836. Dolley returned to Washington in her late years and lived there until her death.

TIME LINE

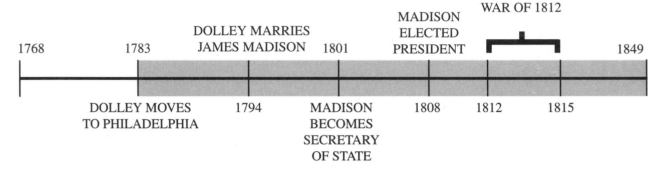

QUESTIONS FOR RESEARCH

1. When and why did the president's house become the White House? Locate some early paintings or engravings of the building. Locate an early painting of Dolley.

2. Research Dolley's more peculiar personal habits. Did she have any?

3. Gilbert Stuart painted a portrait of James Madison, and another of Dolley. Locate a reproduction of each. Did Stuart (or any of his paintings) play a part in the lives of the Madisons? Does a Stuart painting play a part in your life?

NATIONAL STANDARDS CORRELATIONS

NCSS Id: (Culture) Explain why individuals and groups respond differently to their physical and social environments and/or changes to them on the basis of shared assumptions, values, and beliefs.
NSH Era 4, Standard 1: United States territorial expansion between 1801 and 1861, and how it affected relations with external powers and Native Americans

WEBSITES

http://www.americanpresident.org/history/jamesmadison/firstlady/
"First Lady: Dolley Payne Todd Madison," Miller Center for Public Affairs, University of Virginia

http://www.npg.si.edu/cexh/stuart/madison1.htm
"James Madison," Smithsonian National Portrait Gallery

Name: _____   Date: _____

Dolley Madison (cont.)

HISTORICAL FACTS

1. Where was Dolley Madison born? _____

2. In 1790, she married _____. In 1793, both her husband and

    one of her two sons died.

3. She married _____ in 1794, who, at the time of their mar-

    riage, was a congressman from Virginia.

4. James Madison played an important role in the _____,

    although he was overshadowed by Thomas Jefferson.

5. Madison and Hamilton wrote _____ to persuade the nation to

    accept the Constitution.

6. In 1801, President Jefferson appointed Madison to the office of _____

    _____.

7. James Madison became President of the United States. After a hectic first term, war was declared

    on _____ in 1812.

8. The British attacked and burned most of _____.

9. Dolley managed to save a painting of _____ by cutting it

    from its frame.

10. Upon returning to the capital, Dolley quickly reinstituted her elaborate round of _____

    _____.

11. It was some time before an American president could occupy the _____

    _____.

12. Dolley Madison was the first, First Lady to serve _____.

Benjamin Lundy

1789–1839

Benjamin Lundy

Benjamin Lundy was born in Sussex County, New Jersey, the child of Joseph and Eliza Lundy, both of whom were Quakers. Benjamin was given only the barest formal education, and at the age of nineteen, chose to enter the saddler's trade. To learn this, he went to Virginia, where he first came into contact with slavery.

In 1815, he was in Ohio, where he began to organize an anti-slavery society. He was so taken with the goals of abolitionism that he began to contribute articles to various anti-slavery publications. Soon, he closed his saddlery trade and began the publication of his own journal, *The Genius of Universal Emancipation*, which was the forerunner of most influential abolitionist journals of a later time. Lundy had trouble finding a location in which to publish the journal since he was forever meeting opposition. By 1824, he had established his press in Baltimore.

Lundy apparently did not merely want abolition at this stage of his life but became intensely interested as well in the recoloniza-tion of former slaves in Africa. He went to Haiti numerous times in order to find other suitable places in which to colonize African-Americans—each trip resulting in failure.

By this time, Lundy was attracting the interest of pro-slavery groups, and in 1827, he was physi-cally assaulted by a Baltimore slaver as a result of his journal's anti-slavery stand. A year later, Lundy took his crusade to the various northern states in order to curry support. During this trip, he gained the active support of William Lloyd Garrison, a New Englander who joined Lundy in the publication of *The Genius*. But Garrison was so aggressive in his writing that numerous lawsuits were brought against Lundy and his paper, and as a result, he and Garrison soon parted.

It is interesting to note that Lundy operated much in the manner of many early American editors. As he traveled about, he carried some of his printing equipment with him. Then, whenever he had enough material for publication, he had the paper printed in various local printshops. This caused *The Genius* to become so erratic in its appearance that subscriptions dwindled. By 1835, Lundy could no longer keep the paper going even on an irregular basis.

By the mid-1830s, Lundy was in Philadelphia, where he began the publication of another activ-ist journal. His most notable effort during this time was the publication of a pamphlet called *The War in Texas*. Lundy opposed the annexation of Texas and did it so vigorously that he may have been one of the factors in delaying the absorption of the Lone Star Republic.

By this time, he had so many enemies in Pennsylvania that his life was in danger. His personal papers and his equipment were burned by mobs, and he was forced to leave Pennsylvania. He traveled through various parts of the West, helping to organize anti-slavery societies. During this last phase of his life, a few more issues of *The Genius* were published. These last few issues were supposedly printed in Lowell, Illinois—near the town of Hennepin.

Lundy died in 1839, before the abolitionist movement really began to threaten the institution of slavery in a serious way. It must be said, however, that he was a noble pioneer in an attempt to point out the wrongs relating to that sad practice.

Benjamin Lundy (cont.)

TIME LINE

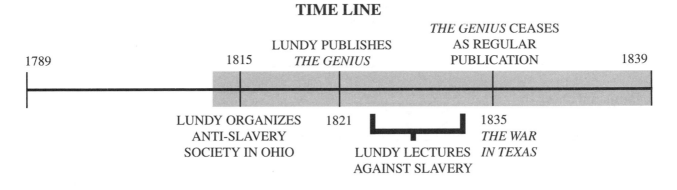

QUESTIONS FOR RESEARCH

1. Trace the relationships between Benjamin Lundy and various other figures of the abolitionist movement—William Lloyd Garrison, Owen and Elijah Lovejoy, and John Brown.

2. What is there in the Quaker faith that caused many of its followers to be abolitionists?

3. At the time, abolitionists were considered radicals. What was the difference in opinion regarding slavery between rank abolitionists such as Garrison and political moderates such as Abraham Lincoln?

NATIONAL STANDARDS CORRELATIONS

NCSS Ve: (Individuals, Groups, & Institutions) Identify and describe examples of tensions between belief systems and government policies and laws.
NSH Era 4, Standard 4: The sources and character of cultural, religious, and social reform movements in the antebellum period

WEBSITES

http://www.ohiohistorycentral.org/ohc/h/peo/lundyb.shtml
"Benjamin Lundy," Ohio Historical Society

http://www.loc.gov/exhibits/african/afam006.html
"Influence of Prominent Abolitionists," The Library of Congress

http://www.nps.gov/boaf/biographies/htm
"Boston African-American National Historic Site: Biographies," National Park Service

Name: _____   Date: _____

Benjamin Lundy (cont.)

HISTORICAL FACTS

1. Benjamin Lundy was born in _____, _____.

2. Benjamin chose the _____ trade.

3. He first came into contact with slavery in Virginia. In 1815, he was in Ohio, where he began to

    organize an _____.

4. Lundy published _____, which was the

    forerunner of the most influential abolitionist journals.

5. Because of the nature of his publication, he had trouble finding a location in which to publish the

    journal. However, by 1824, he had established his press in _____.

6. He also became interested in the _____ of former slaves in

    Africa.

7. He also made several trips to _____ in order to find other

    suitable places to colonize African-Americans.

8. During a crusading trip to the northern states, he gained the active support of _____

    _____.

9. By 1835, Lundy could no longer keep _____ going even on

    an irregular basis.

10. By the mid-1830s, Lundy was in _____, where he began the

    publication of another activist journal.

11. His most notable effort during this time was the pamphlet called _____

    _____.

12. The last few issues of *The Genius* were supposedly printed in _____.

Winfield Scott

1786–1866

Winfield Scott

Winfield Scott was an army officer for over fifty years. He served in three major wars: the War of 1812, the Mexican War, and the Civil War.

Scott was born in Virginia, not far from the very spot at which Robert E. Lee surrendered to General Grant in 1865. He studied at William and Mary College, with the idea of practicing law. That course of life bored him, and in 1808, he joined the U.S. Army. When the War of 1812 broke out, Scott was made a lieutenant colonel and sent to the Canadian border. He was captured at the battle of Queenston Heights but was later exchanged by the British.

Scott was an enormous man. He was well over six feet tall and, at the time of the Civil War, weighed over three hundred pounds. He was a natural for army command from the beginning, and he soon attained the rank of colonel. He carried out a successful campaign to clear the banks of the Niagara River during the War of 1812, which allowed Oliver H. Perry to get his small fleet into Lake Erie. Soon, as a brigadier general, Scott fought two bitter battles—at Chippewa and at Lundy's Lane. He was wounded and carried from the field during the last engagement.

Now, Scott was a national hero, and the state of Virginia granted him a medal. Although the war ended in 1815, Scott stayed with the army and was promoted to the rank of major general. At this time, he composed the manual of arms for the U.S. Army and wrote new versions of infantry tactics to be used by the army. In the early 1840s, he was made the general-in-chief of the army, as well as a lieutenant general.

Scott did such a good job of forming up the army that, when the Mexican War broke out, the regulars performed magnificently. He led one of the American armies in a campaign, and his strong discipline earned him the name of "Old Fuss and Feathers." Despite the implications of the title, Scott's men suffered less from disease and privation than any other command in Mexico.

Scott's invasion of Mexico was one of the greatest campaigns of all time. He landed at Vera Cruz on the Mexican coast and then cut his own communications by marching into the heart of Mexico. There followed a series of battles—Cerro Gordo, Contreras, Churubusco, Molino del Rey, and Chapultepec. Mexico City was finally taken after a valiant defense by the Mexican army. Once Scott captured the Mexican capital, he governed it with such justice that some Mexicans wished him to stay and become emperor of the country.

But Scott was now interested in politics. In 1852, he ran for president as a Whig against Franklin Pierce. Pierce, who had been wounded in Mexico as a volunteer general, had most of the advantages. He had a united Democratic Party, and he was already an experienced politician, while Scott had some of the characteristics of a crusty career general.

With the onset of the Civil War, Scott, who was still in charge of the army, was faced with a dilemma. He was a Virginian, and that state had seceded from the Union. Scott stayed with the Union, however, and organized the forces in 1861. He even devised the Anaconda Plan, which was later applied by President Lincoln against the South. But Scott was old and tired. He was no longer able to operate a field command. Within a few months after the outbreak of the Civil War, Scott retired from the army, but he did live long enough to see a Union victory.

Winfield Scott (cont.)

TIME LINE

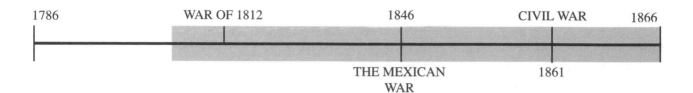

QUESTIONS FOR RESEARCH

1. During the War of 1812, the American army performed poorly. Scott saw this, and was determined to promote a professional officer class. How did he do it?

2. During the Mexican Campaign, Scott was helped by this new class of young officers. Find some of the names of these men, and indicate their importance in later years.

3. What was the Anaconda Plan, and how was it supposed to work? Did it succeed?

NATIONAL STANDARDS CORRELATIONS

NCSS Ie: (Culture) Articulate the implications of cultural diversity, as well as cohesion, within and across groups.

NSH Era 4, Standard 2: How the industrial revolution, increasing immigration, the rapid expansion of slavery, and the westward movement changed the lives of Americans and led toward regional tensions

WEBSITES

http://www.digitalhistory.uh.edu/database/article_display.cfm?HHID=95
"The Anaconda Plan," Digital History

http://www.swcivilwar.com/ScottLetMacWarPlan.html
"General Winfield Scott's Letter to George McClellan describing his general war plan (The Anaconda Plan)," Tim Harrison & The Snuff Works

http://www.almc.army.mil/alog/issues/JanFeb03/MS732.htm
"Logistics Lessons Learned by Lieutenant Grant in Mexico," Logistics Management College, United States Army

Name: _____ Date: _____

Winfield Scott (cont.)

HISTORICAL FACTS

1. Winfield Scott was an army officer for over _____ years.

2. He served in three major wars: the _____, the

   _____, and the _____.

3. Born in Virginia, he studied at _____ and

   _____ College, with the idea of practicing law.

4. In 1808, he joined the U.S. Army. When the War of _____ broke out,

   Scott was made a lieutenant colone!.

5. Captured at the battle of _____, he was later exchanged by

   the _____.

6. Scott was an enormous man. He was well over _____ feet tall and, at the time

   of the Civil War, weighed over _____ pounds.

7. During the War of 1812, Scott became a national hero and was promoted to

   _____.

8. He was wounded at the battle of _____.

9. Scott composed the _____ for the U.S. Army, and

   wrote new versions of _____ to be used by the army.

10. Scott's invasion of _____ was one of the greatest campaigns

    of all time.

11. In 1852, Scott ran unsuccessfully for president as a Whig against _____.

12. Scott was a Virginian, and that state seceded from the Union. He fought for the _____

    in the Civil War.

David Glasgow Farragut

1801–1870

David Glasgow Farragut

David Glasgow Farragut was born near Knoxville, Tennessee, in 1801. He went to sea before he was ten—in fact, he took the name of David after his adoption by the noted naval officer, Captain David Porter. Young Farragut served under Porter as a midshipman during the battle between the USS *Essex* and HMS *Phoebe* and *Cherub*. After a long career in the U.S. Navy, Farragut became a captain in 1855.

His first important action during the Civil War took place in the West. In command of seagoing combat ships, he ordered the bombardment of Vicksburg in 1862. He had managed to bring these larger vessels past the Confederate forts at New Orleans by the daring expedient of sailing past the enemy batteries.

Later, while in command of Gulf squadrons in action against the Confederacy, Farragut chafed at the failure of the Union government to order him against Mobile, a major Confederate stronghold. The naval commander had felt that the expedition would have been successful as early as 1862; but unfortunately, as sometimes happens in war, the national government seemed overcome by the magnitude of its problems. In January 1864, Farragut became so despondent at the lack of direction in naval strategy that he wrote: "I am depressed by the bad news from every direction." Merely patrolling on station outside the entrance to Mobile Bay was not Farragut's idea of warfare.

Finally, in August of 1864, Farragut received the orders he had been waiting for. "I am going into Mobile in the morning, if God is my leader," Farragut wrote his wife. On the morning of August 5, Farragut, now an admiral, told the captain of the *Hartford,* "Well, Drayton, we might as well get under way." His fleet, which consisted of four monitors and fourteen wooden vessels, sailed directly for the entrance of Mobile Bay, which was lined with torpedoes.

Soon the leading monitor, the *Tecumseh*, was sunk by a torpedo. The *Hartford*, with Farragut lashed to the rigging, took the lead. The fleet commander had resorted to this action in order to see over the smoke of battle. It is during this episode that Farragut was supposed to have said, "Damn the torpedoes! Four bells!"—a signal for full speed ahead.

Within three hours, the Confederate ships in the harbor were beaten, and Mobile Bay and the harbor were now under Union control. Of course, the city itself remained Confederate, for Farragut did not have the troops necessary to make a landing. Farragut was now the newest Union hero.

After the defeat of General Hood at Nashville in 1865, Union forces moved freely into the Gulf region. General E.R.S. Canby finally took his blue-coated troopers into Mobile, the last major Confederate fortress to surrender.

Farragut and David D. Porter were the leading naval heroes of the Union in the war. In 1866, Farragut was promoted to the rank of full admiral. He lived four more years.

In a sense, Farragut represents a special type of pre-Civil War naval officer. Virtually raised at sea as a midshipman, Farragut learned his profession in the hard school of reality. After the Civil War, with the growing influence of United States Naval Academy graduates in the fleet, the officer corps of the U.S. Navy was revolutionized in type and personality.

David Glasgow Farragut (cont.)

TIME LINE

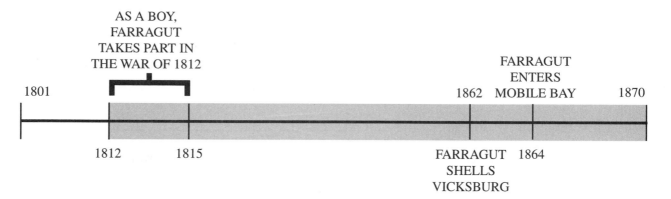

QUESTIONS FOR RESEARCH

1. How did the problem of Mobile and New Orleans fit in with Lincoln's Anaconda Plan?

2. Skimming through your own American history book, how many great American naval commanders can you name? Were any of them similar to Farragut in dash and courage?

3. Where is the U.S. Naval Academy? How does one obtain an appointment to the institution?

4. What was a monitor?

NATIONAL STANDARDS CORRELATIONS

NCSS Vc: (Individuals, Groups, & Institutions) Describe various forms institutions take and the interactions of people with institutions.
NSH Era 5, Standard 2: The course and character of the Civil War and its effects on the American people

WEBSITES

http://www.monitorcenter.org/
"USS Monitor Center," The Mariners' Museum

http://www.digitalhistory.uh.edu/database/article_display.cfm?HHID=95
"The Anaconda Plan," Digital History

http://nautarch.tamu.edu/PROJECTS/denbigh/CoastSurvey.htm
"The U.S. Coast Survey and the Blockade, 1861," The Denbigh Project, Institute of Nautical Archaeology, Texas A & M University

Name: _____ Date: _____

David Glasgow Farragut (cont.)

HISTORICAL FACTS

1. David Glasgow Farragut was born near _____ in 1801.

2. After a long career in the U.S. Navy, Farragut became a _____ in 1855.

3. His first important action during the _____ took place in the West. In command of seagoing combat ships, he ordered the bombardment of _____ in 1863.

4. Later, while in command of Gulf squadrons in action against the _____, Farragut chafed at the failure of his government to order him against Mobile, a major _____ stronghold.

5. When Farragut attacked Mobile, he was _____ to the rigging of his ship, which was named the _____.

6. It is during this episode that Farragut was supposed to have said, "_____ _____."

7. Within three hours, the _____ ships in the harbor were beaten, and the bay and harbor were now under _____ control.

8. After the defeat of _____ at Nashville in 1865, Union forces moved freely into the Gulf Region.

9. General _____ finally took his blue-coated troopers into Mobile, the last major Confederate fortress to surrender.

10. _____ and _____ were the leading naval heroes of the _____ in the War.

11. Farragut was promoted to the rank of _____. He lived four more years.

12. Virtually raised at sea as a midshipman, Farragut learned his profession _____ _____.

Brigham Young

1801–1877

The second president of the Mormon Church was Brigham Young. Young succeeded to the leadership of the Church of Jesus Christ of Latter-Day Saints when Joseph Smith was assassinated in Carthage, Illinois, by elements of a mob.

Brigham Young was born in Vermont. He was taken by his family to western New York where a kind of religious revival was in progress. In 1829, the Youngs settled in Mendon, New York, some forty miles from Palmyra and Fayette where, a year later, Joseph Smith established the Church of the L.D.S. This area has been called by some historians "the burnt-over district," principally because of the intense religious activity found in that section of New York.

The youthful Brigham Young entered into this frenzied activity, and when *The Book of Mormon* was given to him in 1830, he studied it assiduously before eventually becoming an adherent of Smith's new religion. Young never looked back—he never had any doubts as to Smith's divine inspiration. His whole life was devoted to Mormonism.

In 1833, Young led his family and other converts to Kirtland, Ohio, where Mormons had begun to gather after 1830. Young eventually became a member of the Twelve Apostles, an administrative body that assisted Smith in directing the Church.

During these years, Young traveled widely, so that when Smith was killed, it was Young to whom the Apostles turned. By this time, he had contracted three polygamous marriages, a social arrangement that had been "revealed" as proper to Smith. Young assumed leadership at the age of forty-three, a vigorous age for the problems that the Mormons were about to face. Continued battles with non-Mormons ("Gentiles") caused the Mormon leaders to decide upon a mass migration of the sect.

It is not known why Young picked the seemingly barren land near the Great Salt Lake for his settlement. Perhaps he thought it so unattractive that others would not interfere in Mormon life. It is true that the territory belonged to Mexico when the Mormons settled in, but that was changed almost immediately by the American war with Mexico in 1846.

The early years in Salt Lake City (or Deseret) were hard. Plagues of insects plus other difficulties were eventually overcome by luck and pluck. Young himself continued to send out missionaries with great success, especially in the cotton factory areas of England. Many of the converts in Lancashire were of Frisian and Danish antecedents.

What helped the Mormons to succeed in Deseret as much as anything else was the simple fact of the 1849 gold rush. Forty-niners, heading for riches in California, found that Mormon merchants were willing to provide necessities for the last half of their journey at better-than-average prices. The relationships between Mormons and "Gentiles" were often fractious, however, and in 1857, a number of western-bound settlers were massacred by Mormons and Native Americans at Mountain Meadows.

Hard work, luck, and the benefits of irrigation brought wealth to the Mormon farmers, and by 1870, the Mormon colonies had become examples of civic planning and foresight. Polygamy was still

Brigham Young (cont.)

widespread, however, and it was not until 1890 that, on the promise of statehood, the Church changed its doctrine. Finally, it must be added that evangelical work still is an essential part of Mormonism.

Brigham Young died in 1877.

TIME LINE

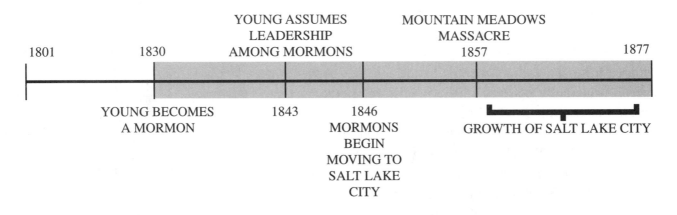

QUESTIONS FOR RESEARCH

1. The principal Mormon city in Illinois in 1840 was Nauvoo. How successful were the Mormons in building this city?

2. What were the reasons for the enmities between Mormons and "Gentiles" during the Mormon Wars?

3. One of the early Mormon names for Utah was Deseret. Where did the name originate, and what was the symbol that Brigham Young always stressed? What is Utah's state symbol today?

NATIONAL STANDARDS CORRELATIONS

NCSS Ve: (Individuals, Groups, & Institutions) Identify and describe examples of tensions between belief systems and government policies and laws.
NSH Era 4, Standard 2: How the industrial revolution, increasing immigration, the rapid expansion of slavery, and the westward movement changed the lives of Americans and led toward regional tensions

WEBSITES

http://www.americaslibrary.gov/cgi-bin/page.cgi/jb/reform/mormon_1
"Brigham Young Settled in the Great Salt Lake Valley July 24, 1847," The Library of Congress

http://www.utah.com/cities/slc_history.htm
"Salt Lake City History," Utah.com

Name: _____ Date: _____

Brigham Young (cont.)

HISTORICAL FACTS

1. The _____ of the Mormon Church was Brigham Young.

2. When _____ was assassinated by a mob in Carthage, Illinois, Young became the leader of the Church of Jesus Christ of Latter-Day Saints.

3. Brigham Young was born in _____.

4. Young had studied _____ in 1830 and eventually became an adherent of Smith's new religion.

5. He led his family, in 1833, and other converts from New York to _____.

6. Young was a member of the _____, an administrative body that assisted Smith in directing the Church.

7. He had _____ polygamous marriages that had been "revealed" as proper to Smith.

8. Mormon leaders decided upon a mass migration to the West, choosing barren land near the _____ for settlement.

9. Plagues of _____ and other difficulties were overcome by the Mormons.

10. The _____ of 1849 helped the Mormons succeed in the desert as much as anything else.

11. In 1857, a number of western-bound settlers were _____ by Mormons and Native Americans at Mountain Meadows.

12. _____ still is an essential part of Mormonism.

Dorothea Lynde Dix

1802–1887

Dorothea Lynde Dix

Dorothea Lynde Dix was born in Hampden, Maine, although she grew up in Massachusetts. Early in her life she was afflicted with a form of tuberculosis, which, although she lived to a ripe old age, troubled her most of her years. She was, from youth on, a kind of semi-invalid who required substantial periods of recuperation. Yet, in spite of this, she was a driving sort of person, and as a young lady became the head of a school for girls. This would have been enough for the ordinary person, but Miss Dix widened her interests to the writing of children's books and to the teaching of women in the East Cambridge House of Corrections.

It was during the latter activity that Dorothea Dix obtained a glimmering of the kind of work to which she should devote her life. To understand this, one has to understand what was happening in the nation as a whole. All over America there was a movement towards reform. Andrew Jackson was a growing force in American politics. Change was in the air, and Dorothea Dix was a product and an instrument of that change. She determined that conditions in the East Cambridge House of Corrections had to be changed, and especially the treatment of the insane had to be humanized. She carried her quest for relief of those insane inmates to Dr. Samuel Gridley Howe, the head of the Perkins Institute for the Blind in Boston. Howe had achieved a national reputation for having successfully trained a blind and deaf mute, Laura Bridgman. Miss Bridgman not only learned to read and write, but became an expert at sewing.

Dr. Howe urged Dorothea Dix to undertake a three-year investigation of the treatment of the insane. This semi-invalid and sometimes ill woman traveled 10,000 miles during this period of time. She visited 300 jails and houses of correction, 500 almshouses, and 18 state prisons.

Her voyage into this previously unexplored world was an astounding one. She found unbelievable conditions—patients chained and locked in closets, patients kept in the filthiest of conditions, and in some cases, insane people who were not allowed to wear clothing. In 1843, at the end of her investigation, she wrote a *Memorial to the Legislature of Massachusetts*. In it she stated:

"I come as the advocate of helpless, forgotten, insane, and idiotic men and women; of beings sunk to a condition from which the most unconcerned would start with real horror; of beings wretched in our prisons, and more wretched in our almshouses."

Through Dorothea Dix's concern, forms of relief were given to the mentally insane. No longer were they kept in prisons along with criminals, but states throughout the nation built asylums for their treatment. From everywhere came support from other reformers and philanthropists. Twenty states and Canada moved to adopt most of her suggestions.

But Dorothea Dix was not yet finished. She visited England, which had similarly bad conditions in its treatment of the insane. She added her voice to the cries of reform there, and changes were eventually made. She traveled throughout much of the world preaching the same gospel, and wherever she went, she found people who listened.

Dorothea Lynde Dix (cont.)

During the American Civil War, Dorothea Dix administered the organization of female nurses for the Union Army. She was exceedingly strict in the administration of rules over these nurses, and she won for female nurses the thanks of a grateful nation.

Miss Dix never married. Despite her periodic bouts with tuberculosis, she lived until 1887—a span of eighty-five years.

TIME LINE

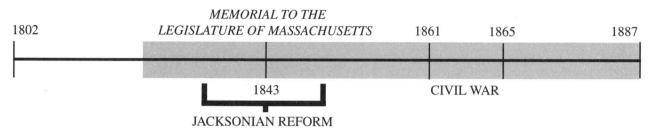

QUESTIONS FOR RESEARCH

1. There were some terrible methods used in the treatment of the insane prior to Dorothea Dix's reform movement. Find some examples of these terrible treatments.

2. Define the word "bedlam." One of the definitions relates to an institution in England. Research that institution.

3. Charles Dickens lived at the same time as Dorothea Dix. Did he write anything about almshouses and the poor?

NATIONAL STANDARDS CORRELATIONS

NCSS IIe: (Time, Continuity, & Change) Develop critical sensitivities such as empathy and skepticism regarding attitudes, values, and behaviors of people in different historical contexts.
NSH Era 4, Standard 4: The sources and character of cultural, religious, and social reform movements in the antebellum period

WEBSITES

http://www.digitalhistory.uh.edu/database/article_display.cfm?HHID=628
"Assisting the Disabled," Digital History

http://www.british-history.ac.uk/report.asp?compid=35362
"Houses of Military Orders: St. Mary of Bethlehem," University of London & History of Parliament Trust

http://www.webster.edu/~woolflm/dorotheadix.html
"Dorothea Dix," Webster University

Name: _____ Date: _____

Dorothea Lynde Dix (cont.)

HISTORICAL FACTS

1. Dorothea Lynde Dix was born in _____, although she grew up in _____.

2. Early in her life she was afflicted with a form of _____, which made her a semi-invalid for the rest of her life.

3. As a young lady, Dix became the head of a _____.

4. She also became interested and involved in a number of things. She determined that conditions in the _____ had to be changed, and that especially the treatment of the _____ had to be humanized.

5. Dr. Samuel Gridley Howe, head of the Perkins Institute for the Blind, urged Dorothea Dix to undertake a _____ of the treatment of the insane.

6. In her investigation, she traveled 10,000 miles and visited _____, _____, and _____.

7. In 1843, at the end of her investigation, she wrote _____ _____.

8. Through Dorothea Dix's concern, forms of relief were given to the _____.

9. No longer were they treated as criminals, but states built _____ for their treatment.

10. She visited _____, where changes were eventually made for the better.

11. During the Civil War, Dorothea Dix administered the organization of female nurses for the _____ army.

12. Miss Dix never married. Despite her periodic bouts with a terrible disease, she lived _____ years.

George Thomas

1816–1870

There are many historians who contend that the most under-credited general in the Civil War was George Thomas. There is considerable substance to their arguments, because only twice during the war were Confederate troops completely routed in battle. In both instances, George Thomas was the general in charge of the Union forces opposing them.

George Thomas

It should be noted that Thomas was southern born. When he decided to stay with the Union in 1861, his family cut him off from all communication. He became, to them, someone who had never existed. Because he was born in Virginia, he was never allowed the confidence that should have been accorded him by other Northern officers. Every promotion that he achieved was won by almost superhuman effort.

Thomas won some early victories in the war, which, though minor in scope, served to buoy a depressed Union. Despite these successes, he was made a subordinate of General Don Carlos Buell, to whom he was easily superior in abilities. At Perryville in Kentucky and near Murfreesboro in Tennessee, he proved to be solid and able in defense. In the fall of 1863, General Rosecrans, now Thomas's superior, moved the Army of the Cumberland farther into Tennessee and towards Georgia. The Union troops captured Chattanooga, but on September 19 and 20, General Bragg and a Confederate army opened a series of vicious attacks upon Rosecrans's lines, which had been situated near Chickamauga Creek.

On the second day of these battles, Rosecrans's lines crumbled and a large part of the army fled to Chattanooga. It was a rout, but it might have become a disaster if Thomas, who was holding the Union's left, had not continued to fight. Throughout the late afternoon of the 20th, Bragg tried to break Thomas's hold on the ridge running along the Union lines. Attack after attack was thrown back. Not only did Thomas blunt the will of the Confederates to fight any longer, but he allowed the remainder of the Union army to flee to Chattanooga where it could regroup.

But once again Thomas was not given the command of the attempt to break out of Chattanooga—U.S. Grant was. On November 23 and 25, Grant ordered a series of attacks, placing the major responsibility with his own favorite commander, W.T. Sherman. Thomas's troops were merely ordered to occupy the lower trenches of Missionary Ridge.

In the battles that ensued, Sherman failed to occupy his objective, but Thomas's troops stormed so angrily up Missionary Ridge that they routed the Confederate defenders. Thomas had won the day, but Grant got the public credit.

Later, Thomas and his Army of the Cumberland, along with the Union Army of the Tennessee, were commanded by General William T. Sherman. Once again, in the drive to Atlanta, Thomas fought magnificently. But after the capture of the city, he was sent back to guard Nashville, Tennessee, with some of the worst regiments under Sherman's command. General Hood, with his Confederate army, invaded Nashville, and it seemed for a while as if Thomas would be overwhelmed. Distrusted by Grant, hounded by the press, and caught with bad weather, Thomas finally attacked Hood on December 15 and 16, 1864, and almost obliterated the southern force.

George Thomas (cont.)

In the final analysis, Thomas always seemed subordinate to the figures of Grant, Sherman, and Sheridan. Years after the war, when Thomas was visiting New Orleans, General Hood called to pay a friendly visit. After a short visit, Hood left the room in tears, saying, "If Thomas had only been on our side, we would have won the war."

TIME LINE

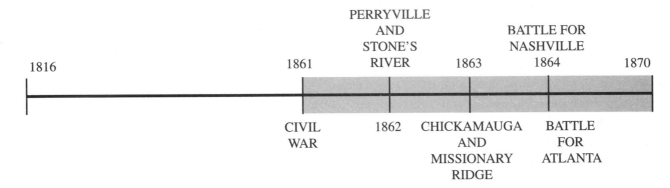

QUESTIONS FOR RESEARCH

1. During the Battle of Chickamauga, General Rosecrans made a serious but understandable mistake at the end of the first day. What was it, and how did it affect the battle?

2. Research Thomas's Civil War career to find a military defeat in his record.

3. Thomas's personality—what was it like? Does it fit the name given to him by people of the Union during the war—"The Rock of Chickamauga"?

NATIONAL STANDARDS CORRELATIONS

NCSS VIf: (Power, Authority, & Governance) Explain conditions, actions, and motivations that contribute to conflict and cooperation within and among nations.
NSH Era 5, Standard 2: The course and character of the Civil War and its effects on the American people

WEBSITES

http://www.americaslibrary.gov/cig-bin/page.cgi/jb/nation/chickamauga_1
"General George H. Thomas, Rock of Chickamauga," The Library of Congress

http://www.swcivilwar.com/thomas.html
"Major General George Thomas," Tim Harrison & The Snuff Works

Name: _____   Date: _____

George Thomas (cont.)

HISTORICAL FACTS

1. There are many historians who contend that the most under-credited general in the Civil War was

    _____.

2. Thomas was _____ born.

3. He was born in _____ in 1816.

4. In the fall of 1863, _____, now Thomas's superior, moved the

    Army of the Cumberland farther into _____ and toward Georgia.

5. The Union troops captured _____.

6. In the battle of _____ Creek, Rosecrans's lines crumbled; however,

    _____ lines continued to fight, preventing a complete

    disaster.

7. Thomas allowed the remainder of the Union Army to flee to _____

    where it could regroup.

8. But once again Thomas was not given the command of the attempt to break out of Chattanooga—

    _____ was.

9. The general ordered a series of attacks, placing the major responsibility with his own favorite

    commander, _____.

10. Thomas's troops stormed so angrily up _____ that they

    routed the Confederate defenders.

11. After a successful battle at Atlanta, he was sent back to guard Nashville.

    _____, with his Confederate army, was defeated by Thomas

    on December 15 and 16, 1864. This almost obliterated the southern force.

12. In the final analysis, Thomas always seemed subordinate to the figures of

    _____, _____, and

    _____.

Philip Henry Sheridan

1831–1888

Philip Henry Sheridan

What a feisty little military leader this man was! He was Irish by origin, probably born in County Cavan. His mother brought him to Ohio where he was reared. Unfortunately, little is known of this stage of his life, although there was obviously enough political leverage in his family to obtain his appointment to the United States Military Academy.

Philip Henry Sheridan was therefore in line for quick military promotion at the outbreak of the Civil War. He moved from the rank of captain to that of brigadier general in a short span of time. He commanded a division at Perryville, Kentucky, where a hard battle against Confederate troops took place. At Stone's River, he performed brilliantly and helped to save the day for Rosecrans's Union Army in Tennessee. At Chickamauga, a terrible Union defeat, he fought hard to maintain his position, but like others, his command was swept aside by the Confederate onrush. Shortly thereafter, he led an assault on Missionary Ridge and helped to drive the Confederates off in a rout.

When U.S. Grant was called east to take command of the entire Union army, he took Sheridan with him. During the Union campaign against Lee in Virginia in 1864, Sheridan was given the arduous task of guarding communications. Later, he swept through the Shenandoah Valley, destroying the economic resources of the region. When General Jubal Early of the Confederacy made a surprise attack against Sheridan's forces, the Union general made a long ride to rejoin his troops and to rally them at Cedar Creek. Thomas Read later celebrated this exploit with the poem "Sheridan's Ride." Read did make a mistake in the factual content of the poem, however, by giving Sheridan credit for riding more miles than he really did.

Sheridan was now involved in the closing Union ring around Lee. The vital event in this last great campaign was Sheridan's victory at Five Forks. Lee was forced to leave his trenches, and the great Southern leader was brought to bay at Appomattox.

Sheridan was a major general at the end of the war, and in 1865, he was given the task of commanding the Division of the Gulf. While there, he prepared his forces for a possible attempt to drive the French from Mexico. Fortunately, this necessity was eliminated when the French army sailed back to Europe.

During the Reconstruction period, Sheridan was given command of the Fifth Military District (Louisiana and Texas). Later, in command of the Department of the Missouri, he directed campaigns against hostile Native American tribes. A lieutenant general in 1869, he went to Europe and observed the conduct of the Franco-Prussian War. In 1884, he succeeded William T. Sherman as the Commander of the Army, and in 1888, he was made a full general. This was the last year of his life. In anticipation of his death, he hastily wrote his *Personal Memoirs*. He is buried in the National Cemetery at Arlington.

Philip Henry Sheridan (cont.)

TIME LINE

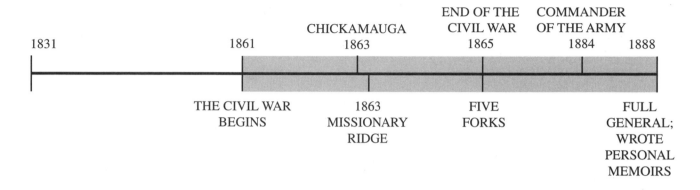

QUESTIONS FOR RESEARCH

1. Why was it important for the Union Army to have a general of Irish origins in an important position of command?

2. What were the qualities of command that caused Sheridan to be of importance to Grant and to the Union cause?

3. What were the French doing in Mexico, and why was it necessary to force them out?

NATIONAL STANDARDS CORRELATIONS

NCSS VIf: (Power, Authority, & Governance) Explain conditions, actions, and motivations that contribute to conflict and cooperation within and among nations.

NSH Era 5, Standard 2: The course and character of the Civil War and its effects on the American people

WEBSITES

http://ehistory.osu.edu/world/PeopleView.Cfm?PID=65
"Philip H. Sheridan, (Little Phil)," The Ohio State University

http://www.pbs.org/weta/thewest/people/s_z/sheridan.htm
"Philip Henry Sheridan (1831–1888)," The West Film Project and WETA

http://www.army.mil.cmh-pg/books/cg&csa/Sheridan-PH.htm
"Philip Henry Sheridan," United States Army Center of Military History

http://www.tsha.utexas.edu/handbook/online/articles/SS/fsh26.html
"Sheridan, Philip Henry," The Texas State Historical Association

Name: _____   Date: _____

Philip Henry Sheridan (cont.)

HISTORICAL FACTS

1. Sheridan was Irish by origin, born in _____ and reared in

    Ohio.

2. He was educated at the _____.

3. Philip Henry Sheridan was therefore in line for quick military promotion at the outbreak of the

    _____.

4. He moved from the rank of captain to that of _____ in a short

    span of time.

5. At Stone's River, he performed brilliantly, and he helped to save the day for _____

    Union Army in Tennessee.

6. At _____, a terrible Union defeat, he fought hard to maintain

    his position; but like others, his command was swept aside by the Confederate onrush.

7. He led an assault on _____ and helped to drive the Confeder-

    ates off in a rout.

8. When _____ was called to take command of the entire Union

    Army, he took Sheridan with him.

9. His troops swept through the _____, destroying the economic

    resources of the region.

10. Sheridan was involved in closing the Union ring around _____.

11. Sheridan was a _____ at the end of the war, and in 1865, was

    given the task of commanding the _____.

12. During the _____, Sheridan was given command of the Fifth

    Military District (Louisiana and Texas). Later in command of the Department of the Missouri, he

    directed campaigns against _____.

Helen Hunt Jackson

1830–1885

Helen Hunt Jackson, who was born in Amherst, Massachu-setts, in 1830, was known as the foremost advocate of justice for Native Americans during the nineteenth century. After the Civil War, the impetus to "go West" was given added force by the discovery of rich silver and gold deposits in the Dakotas, Colorado, and Ne-vada. The addition of the transcontinental railroad—the union of the Union Pacific and the Central Pacific—erased the necessity of long and arduous passages over the Great Plains. The days of the independent Native American tribes were almost finished.

Yet Native Americans did not give up easily. By the end of the Civil War, there were approximately 275,000 Native Americans west of the Mississippi. The major tribes who comprised this total included the Sioux, the Crow, and the Blackfeet, located in the Dakotas and Montana; the Cheyenne, the Kiowa, and the Apache in the American Southwest; and the Ute, the Snake, and the Bannock in the central area of the Great Plains.

Prior to the war, the white frontier had moved into specific areas in Wyoming, Kansas, Nebraska, and the Dakotas. During the war, when the Union Army was engaged in a life and death struggle with the Confederacy, the Native Americans took advantage of the scarcity of troops and attacked certain white settlements in the West. In 1862, the Sioux attacked settlers in Minnesota and, with a savagery scarcely equaled anywhere in the West, killed 450 whites. Two years later, the Cheyenne and the Arapaho at-tacked on the Colorado frontier, causing great loss of life. The retaliation by American military forces was likewise savage in its nature.

At the time, to many of the leading American military commanders, there seemed no adequate solution except complete submission on the part of the Native Americans—or the complete annihilation of all "hostile" tribes. Time and again, the Native Americans struck back—each time to be severely pun-ished by retaliatory army action. The massacre of Colonel Custer's 265 men at the Little Bighorn was only a temporary interlude. In the end, the Native Americans were thoroughly overwhelmed.

With the end of the Indian Wars, the various tribes either drifted onto barren and unproductive reservations, or they slowly melted away before the fundamental changes that were occurring on the frontier. The buffalo had disappeared—that was one change—and disease and whiskey scourged almost all tribes, weakening tribal independence.

More and more, there were some Americans who objected to what they considered ill-treatment of Native Americans. Helen Hunt Jackson was one of these Americans. In 1881, she wrote *A Century of Dishonor*, a highly overstated but effective case for the Native Americans. In the book, she charged the American government with mismanagement of Indian affairs. To make her arguments stronger, she sent a copy of her book to every member of Congress. As a result, she was appointed special commissioner to investigate Indian affairs management. Three years later, in 1884, she wrote one of the most popular novels of her time—*Ramona*.

Unfortunately, the condition of the Native Americans was scarcely improved for the next century. But one cannot fault Helen Hunt Jackson for trying.

Helen Hunt Jackson (cont.)

TIME LINE

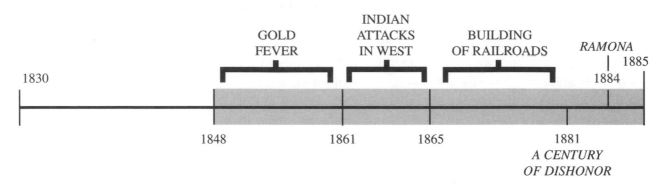

QUESTIONS FOR RESEARCH

1. Not all Native American tribes were pushed off their lands completely. Find some examples of Native Americans still living on or near tribal lands in states east of the Mississippi.

2. Native Americans have fought well for the United States in World Wars I and II, the Korean War, and the Vietnam War. Find the names of some of these heroes.

3. It is true that the American army committed misdeeds against Native Americans in the West. Are there examples of the reverse? How many Native Americans are there today as compared to 1870?

NATIONAL STANDARDS CORRELATIONS

NCSS Vf: (Individuals, Groups, & Institutions) Describe the role of institutions in furthering both continuity and change.
NSH Era 6, Standard 4: Federal Indian policy and United States foreign policy after the Civil War

WEBSITES

http://memory.loc.gov/cgi-bin/ampage?collId=llss&fileName=4000/4015/llss4015.db&recNum=129
"A Century of Lawmaking for a New Nation: United States Congressional Documents and Debates, 1774–1875," The Library of Congress

http://www.history.navy.mil/faqs/faq61-3.htm
"American Indian Medal of Honor Winners," Naval Historical Center, Department of the Navy

http://www.cogreatwomen.org/jackson/htm
"Helen Hunt Jackson," Colorado Women's Hall of Fame

http://hdl.loc.gov/loc.gmd/g4051e.mf000045
"Indian Reservations West of the Mississippi River," The Library of Congress

Name: _____ Date: _____

Helen Hunt Jackson (cont.)

HISTORICAL FACTS

1. Helen Hunt Jackson was born in _____ in _____.

2. After the Civil War, the impetus to "go West" was given added force by the discovery of rich _____ and _____ deposits in the _____, _____, and _____.

3. The addition of the transcontinental railroad—the union of the _____ and the _____—eased the necessity of long and arduous passages over the Great Plains.

4. The days of the independent _____ were almost finished.

5. By the end of the Civil War, there were approximately _____ Native Americans west of the Mississippi.

6. The major tribes included the _____, the _____, and _____, located in the Dakotas and Montana; the _____, the _____, and _____, in the American Southwest; and the _____, the _____, and the _____ in the central area of the Great Plains.

7. When the Union Army was engaged in a life and death struggle with the Confederacy, the Native Americans took advantage of the _____ and attacked certain white settlements.

8. In 1862, the Sioux attacked settlers in Minnesota and, with a savagery scarcely equaled anywhere in the West, killed _____ whites. Two years later, the _____ and the _____ attacked on the Colorado frontier, causing great loss of life.

9. The Massacre of _____'s 265 men at the Little Bighorn was only a temporary interlude. In the end, the Native Americans were thoroughly overwhelmed.

10. The tribes declined partly because the _____ had disappeared, and _____ and _____ had weakened tribal independence.

11. Helen Hunt Jackson objected to the ill-treatment of Native Americans. In 1881, she wrote the book _____.

12. She was appointed _____ to investigate Indian affairs management.

Blanche K. Bruce

1841–1898

Senator Blanche Bruce

Here is one of the more interesting lives in this gallery of "great Americans." There are contradictions, surprises, and pleasing revelations in the singular story of Blanche K. Bruce.

Bruce was an African-American who was born into slavery in Farmville, Prince Edward County, Virginia, on March 1, 1841. Very little is known of his childhood. However, unlike most slaves, he was tutored by his master's son. All of the slaveholders in Virginia were not white—a surprising number were African-American, so perhaps that was the case with Bruce.

Bruce's family moved to Missouri when Bruce was a boy. He later attended Oberlin College in Ohio for two years, where he took what might be called a general education curriculum. Oberlin, incidentally, was the first co-racial college in the United States and was in the business of educating African-Americans before the Civil War. For a time, Bruce taught school in Hannibal, Missouri.

In 1868, after the South was reoccupied through the Military Reconstruction Act, Bruce appeared in Mississippi, where he not only became a plantation owner but an owner of considerable property as well. He also taught for a while and engaged himself in the search for political office. He moved through the office of tax assessor, sheriff of Bolivar County, and the Board of Levee Commissioners of Mississippi. In 1874, he was elected to the United States Senate from Mississippi.

Bruce served in the Senate for six years—to the actual end of Reconstruction—and as a legislator he compiled an interesting record. He was involved in numerous debates over election frauds and civil rights in the South. He opposed the various policies designed to keep Chinese immigrants from American shores and took the side of the Native Americans in various struggles with Federal power. He even worked to obtain a form of amnesty for ex-Confederates in Mississippi.

One of his major concerns seems to have been federal aid in harnessing the Mississippi River. He worked for flood control and the improvement of navigation facilities, and he argued that foreign commerce should be encouraged to enter various ports along the river.

When Reconstruction ended, so did Bruce's senatorial career. He stayed on in Washington, however, and President Garfield made him the Registrar of the Treasury, a position he held until 1885. In 1889, President Harrison appointed him Recorder of Deeds in the District of Columbia. This was not an insignificant position. Still later, after the election of President McKinley, Bruce was once again made the Registrar of the Treasury. He died in 1898.

Blanche K. Bruce (cont.)

TIME LINE

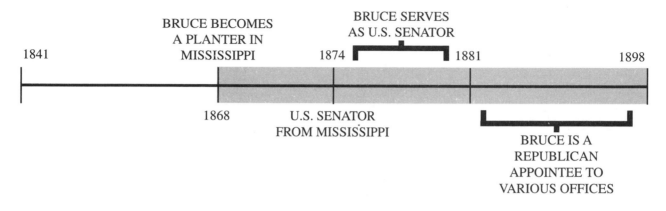

QUESTIONS FOR RESEARCH

1. Does it surprise you that African-Americans were attending some colleges before 1860? John Hope Franklin has written much on the history of African-Americans. Find the names of some pre-Civil War African-Americans who were highly educated.

2. Does it surprise you that African-Americans could be slaveholders in some southern states? Were there many? Were there Native American plantation owners who also owned slaves? J. G. Randall, in his *Civil War and Reconstruction*, has some information on this.

3. Explain why Bruce could be elected as a senator from Mississippi in 1874. Are there many African-American senators today?

NATIONAL STANDARDS CORRELATIONS

NCSS Ve: (Individuals, Groups, & Institutions) Identify and describe examples of tensions between belief systems and government policies and laws.
NSH Era 5, Standard 3: How various Reconstruction plans succeeded or failed.

WEBSITES

http://bioguide.congress.gov/scripts/biodisplay.pl?index=B000968
"BRUCE, Blanche Kelso (1841–1898)," Biographical Directory of the United States Congress

http://odur.let.rug.nl/~usa/D/1876-1900/reconstruction/bruce.htm
"Blanche K. Bruce: Speech in Senate March 31, 1876," Department of Humanities Computing, University of Groningen, The Netherlands

http://www.uga.edu/~iaas/History.html
"Benjamin Banncker," Institute for African American Studies, The University of Georgia

Name: _____   Date: _____

Blanche K. Bruce (cont.)

HISTORICAL FACTS

1. Bruce was an African-American born into slavery in Farmville, Prince Edward County,

   _____, on March 1, 1841.

2. Bruce's family moved to _____ when he was a boy.

3. He took a general education curriculum the two years he attended Oberlin College in Ohio. This

   was the first _____ college in the United States.

4. Bruce moved to Mississippi in 1868 where he became a _____ owner.

5. He was a teacher for a while and a _____.

6. In 1874, he was elected to the _____ from Mississippi.

7. He championed _____ in the United States, opposing policies

   designed to keep Chinese immigrants from America, and took the side of Native Americans.

8. Bruce worked to obtain a form of _____ for ex-Confederates

   in Mississippi.

9. He worked hard for _____ in harnessing the Mississippi River.

10. Working for _____ control and the improvement of

    _____, he argued that foreign commerce should be encour-

    aged to use the ports along the river.

11. When the _____ era ended, so did Bruce's senatorial career;

    however, he remained in Washington.

12. He was _____ to various federal positions by Presidents Gar-

    field, Harrison, and McKinley.

Justin Smith Morrill

1810–1898

If one were to ask the ordinary American citizen to identify Justin Smith Morrill, the chances are that he would receive a blank stare in response. Yet, in fact, Morrill was one of the most important factors in American growth in the nineteenth century. His contributions still are.

Justin Smith Morrill

Justin Morrill was born in Vermont in 1810. He received the ordinary education of the time—the village school and local academies. At fifteen years of age, he became a store clerk, an occupation that he followed until 1828. Soon he was a partner in a local store and prospered so much in the enterprise that he was able to retire in 1848 at a young age.

Now married, he entered into local politics with zest. He served on county and state committees, and in 1852, he attended the Whig convention as a delegate. This was the last gasp of a dying Whig Party, and in 1854, Morrill entered Congress as one of the few remaining members of that party. Soon, with the expiration of the Whigs, Morrill moved into the newly formed Republican Party.

His public life constitutes a kind of record for service. He represented constituents for six terms in the House, and in 1866, he was elected to the Senate, where his term of service was almost thirty-two years.

His committee assignments were varied and important during this time. He was a member of the Ways and Means Committee, served as Chairman of the Committee on Finance, and pushed the principle of abolition. As a member of the Ways and Means Committee, Morrill wrote a bill that eventually became known as the Morrill Tariff Act. His greatest accomplishment was the famous Land-Grant College Act, although the passage of the Act did not come easily. Morrill introduced the Land-Grant Act in 1857, but it took two years for the bill to go through both Houses. Then, in 1859, President Buchanan vetoed the first version of the Act.

With southern opposition gone during the Civil War, President Lincoln signed the bill in 1862. What the Morrill Act did was to provide a Federal land grant equal to 30,000 acres to every state for each senator or representative to which it was entitled under the census of 1860. In other words, if a state was entitled to two representatives and two senators, then it would receive 120,000 acres. The income derived from the sale of these lands by each state was to be used for "the endowment, support, and maintenance of at least one college where the leading object shall be, without excluding other scientific and classical studies, and including military tactics, to teach such branches of learning as are related to agriculture and mechanic arts ..."

Western states were the first to accept public lands for educational purposes. State universities were created in Kansas (1864), Illinois (1867), Minnesota (1868), and California (1868). One of the earlier eastern schools to accept public funds on the basis of the Morrill Act was Cornell University.

The old "land-grant" universities have served the country well, both in providing education for the masses and in developing new techniques in industry, farming, and commerce. Agriculture alone has been revolutionized through innovations and discoveries made at these universities.

Justin Smith Morrill (cont.)

What happened to Morrill after 1862? He pushed through a Second Morrill Act in 1890, which increased the amount of money available to land-grant schools. He was also responsible for the beautification of Washington, D.C., in the 1890s. This man's long career in public service ended when he died in 1898.

TIME LINE

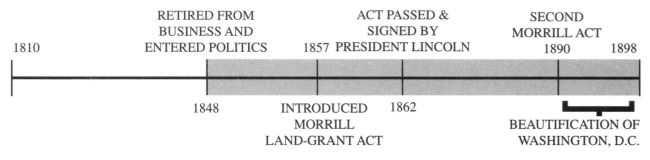

QUESTIONS FOR RESEARCH

1. How unusual was it for a nation to finance its educational growth in the manner in which the United States did in the 1860s? How was higher education financed in England, France, and Germany during the same period?

2. Can you discover some of the circumstances of the founding of your state university? Was it a land-grant school? Some states did not have state universities as such until the 1960s. Which states were they?

3. The earliest land-grant schools placed heavy stress on what subjects? List courses taught in your state university in its earlier years.

NATIONAL STANDARDS CORRELATIONS

NCSS Ve: (Individuals, Groups, & Institutions) Identify and describe examples of tensions between belief systems and government policies and laws.
NSH Era 4, Standard 4: The sources and character of cultural, religious, and social reform movements in the antebellum period

WEBSITES

http://bioguide.congress.gov/scripts/biodisplay.pl?index=M000969
"MORRILL, Justin Smith (1810–1898)," Biographical Directory of the United States Congress

http://www.loc.gov/rr/program/bib/ourdocs/Morrill.html
"Morrill Act," The Library of Congress

Name: _____   Date: _____

Justin Smith Morrill (cont.)

HISTORICAL FACTS

1. Justin Morrill was born in _____ in 1810.

2. At age 15, he became a _____.

3. He soon was a partner in a local store where he did very well, retiring at age _____.

4. In 1854, Morrill entered _____ as one of the last members of the Whig Party.

5. The Whig Party soon expired, and Morrill moved into the newly formed _____ Party.

6. He represented constituents for _____ terms in the House.

7. In 1866, he was elected to the Senate, where his term of service was almost _____ years.

8. As a member of the _____ Committe, Morril wrote a bill that eventually became known as the Morrill Tariff Act.

9. His greatest accomplishment was the famous _____ College Act.

10. In 1859, President Buchanan _____ the first version of the Act.

11. President Lincoln signed the bill in _____.

12. This bill provided a federal land grant equal to _____ acres to every state for each senator and representative to which it was entitled under the census of 1860.

13. The money from the sale of these lands was to be used for the endowment of at least one college in the state, called "_____ universities."

14. _____ alone has been revolutionized through innovations and discoveries made at these universities.

Elizabeth Cady Stanton

1815–1902

Elizabeth Cady Stanton was one of the great women of the Victorian era. She was born in 1815, the year the War of 1812 ended. She grew up in a very religious atmosphere; her parents seemed to inspire fear rather than love in the child. It is probable that Simon Hosack, a minister of the Presbyterian Church, had a greater influence on Elizabeth than her parents. Hosack pushed Elizabeth into pursuing an education superior to that acquired by most girls of her time. She studied Greek, Latin, and mathematics, and in each field achieved high marks.

Elizabeth Cady Stanton

When Elizabeth was fifteen, she was sent to a girls' school operated by Emma Willard in Troy, New York. She graduated from that institution in 1832 and then entered into the study of law. She quickly learned that there were enormous handicaps placed upon the professional advancement of women. At this stage of her life, she fell under the influence of reformer Gerrit Smith, who ignited her interest in the temperance and anti-slavery movements.

In 1840, she married Henry Brewster Stanton, and during the ceremony, the word *obey* was omitted from the marriage vows. Stanton, who was a noted reformer himself, soon thereafter attended a world anti-slavery conference in London. Elizabeth accompanied him, and while there, met Lucretia Coffin Mott. Mrs. Mott and others were refused official recognition by the conference, and as a consequence, both Mrs. Mott and Mrs. Stanton were determined to organize a women's rights convention.

The goal of this Victorian women's liberation movement was delayed for some time. The convention was finally held in 1848, in the Wesleyan Methodist Church in Seneca Falls, New York. Through the insistence of Elizabeth Cady Stanton, a resolution calling for women's suffrage was adopted.

Now Mrs. Stanton began to give more and more of her time to the cause of women—to lecturing, writing, and organizing local feminist groups. In 1851, she met Susan B. Anthony and persuaded her to enter the fight for women's rights. The two women were an ideal team. Mrs. Stanton was more voluble, but Susan B. Anthony had more patience and organizational ability.

Mrs. Stanton's aims covered the areas of divorce, suffrage, and professional rights. In 1869, she helped organize the National American Woman Suffrage Association and was consequently chosen as its first president. This was the most radical of women's organizations, and Mrs. Stanton filled the presidency for twenty-one years.

Amazingly, Mrs. Stanton was able to balance domestic demands with her personal goals. She bore seven children; yet she devoted eight months every year to lecturing throughout the states of the union. In 1868, she joined in the establishment of *Revolution*, a magazine devoted to women's rights. She also wrote for the *North American Review*, one of America's oldest and most respected magazines.

In 1898, when she was drawing to the close of her career, she published her own life story—*Eighty Years and More*. But even then, she was not quite finished. Along with Susan B. Anthony and Matilda Joslyn Gage, she helped to produce three enormous volumes on the *History of Woman Suffrage*. She died in 1902. However, the movement that she helped to begin still continues.

Elizabeth Cady Stanton (cont.)

TIME LINE

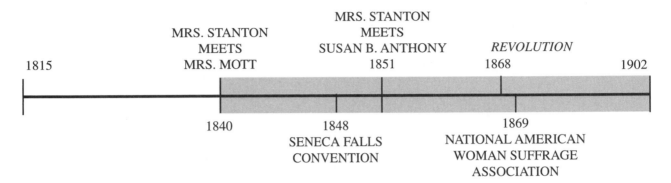

QUESTIONS FOR RESEARCH

1. Describe the reaction of many American men to the Seneca Falls Convention of 1848.

2. In what ways did the women's rights movement of Mrs. Stanton's time fit into the period of Jacksonian reform? What other great reform movements were there?

3. Find the names of some American women who successfully entered professions after 1865.

NATIONAL STANDARDS CORRELATIONS

NCSS Ve: (Individuals, Groups, & Institutions) Identify and describe examples of tensions between belief systems and government policies and laws.

NSH Era 4, Standard 4: The sources and character of cultural, religious, and social reform movements in the antebellum period

WEBSITES

http://www.nps.gov/wori/ecs.htm
"Elizabeth Cady Stanton," National Park Service

http://memory.loc.gov/ammem/naw/nawshome.html
"Selections from the National American Woman Suffrage Association Collection 1848–1921," The Library of Congress

http://ecssba.rutgers.edu/docs/ecswoman1.html
"Address by Elizabeth Cady Stanton on Woman's Rights," Rutgers, The State University of New Jersey

Name: _____   Date: _____

Elizabeth Cady Stanton (cont.)

HISTORICAL FACTS

1. Elizabeth Cady Stanton was one of the great women of the _____ era.

2. Stanton studied Greek, Latin, and mathematics. When she was fifteen, she was sent to a girls' school operated by _____ in Troy, New York, where she graduated in 1832 and then entered the study of _____.

3. She fell under the influence of reformer Gerrit Smith, who ignited her interest in the _____ and anti-slavery movements.

4. In 1840, she married Henry Brewster Stanton, and during the ceremony the word "_____" was omitted from the marriage vows.

5. Elizabeth went with her husband to London to attend a world anti-slavery conference; while there she met _____.

6. Mrs. Mott and others were refused official recognition by the conference, and as a consequence, both Mrs. Mott and _____ were determined to organize a women's rights convention.

7. This convention was delayed until 1848. It was held in the Wesleyan Methodist Church in Seneca Falls, New York. A resolution calling for _____ was adopted.

8. In 1851, Mrs. Stanton met _____ and persuaded her to enter the fight for women's rights.

9. Mrs. Stanton's aims covered the areas of _____, _____, and _____.

10. Mrs. Stanton helped organize the _____ Association, where she was president for twenty-one years.

11. Mr. and Mrs. Stanton had _____ children, yet she devoted eight months each year to lecturing throughout the states of the union.

12. Along with Susan B. Anthony and Matilda Joslyn Gage, she helped to produce three enormous volumes on the _____.

Carl Schurz

1829–1906

Carl Schurz

Carl Schurz deserves a higher place in American history than he is normally given. He was born in Prussia and attended the University of Bonn. He was involved in the 1848 German revolutions, and after their failure, he came to the United States. Settling in Wisconsin, he soon began to make his presence felt in his new land. He had married a German-Jewish girl who had studied the process of education in Europe. Encouraged by Schurz, she introduced the kindergarten idea to this country. Schurz himself became involved in the anti-slavery movement. In 1860, he worked diligently on Lincoln's presidential campaign and was rewarded with an appointment as the U.S. Minister to Spain. President Lincoln also made him a brigadier general in the Union Army, and even though his military record was undistinguished, he managed to keep German-Americans strongly behind the cause.

Following the Civil War, Schurz became the editor of the very powerful German-language newspaper, the *Westliche Post* of St. Louis. It is interesting to note that one of the men employed during this time by Schurz was another German immigrant, Joseph Pulitzer.

As an editor, Schurz became concerned with corruption and reform. He led most of the Illinois and Missouri German-Americans into the Liberal Republican Party of 1872, and he backed Horace Greeley against his old commander, Ulysses S. Grant.

The election was a bitter one, and Greeley, who was a poor choice, campaigned widely throughout the land. He almost lost the German-American vote completely—despite Schurz's backing—when he announced his belief in the temperance movement. Of course, Greeley lost.

The way back into national politics was not easy for Schurz. He had backed the wrong candidate in the 1872 election, and in politics, loyalty is considered a most prime requisite. Nevertheless, Schurz used the springboard of a Senate position from Missouri to push for the election of the reform-minded presidential candidate in 1876—Rutherford B. Hayes.

This time, Schurz's man won, and in 1877, the German-American became the secretary of the interior. In this position, he pushed for fair treatment of Native Americans and for the introduction of a most revolutionary reform notion—the civil service system.

Eventually civil service did come—in the Chester Arthur administration—and even though it did not accomplish much in the beginning, it was a start towards eliminating some parts of the spoils system operating at that time.

Schurz's major contributions in politics were now over. He became the editor of the New York *Evening Post* in 1892 and, still later, an editorial writer for *Harper's Weekly*.

What happened to Schurz's old employee, Joseph Pulitzer? He eventually bought the *St. Louis Dispatch*, which was later combined with another paper called the *Post*. Using the *Post-Dispatch* as a base, Pulitzer then bought the *New York World*, as well as other papers.

Carl Schurz (cont.)

TIME LINE

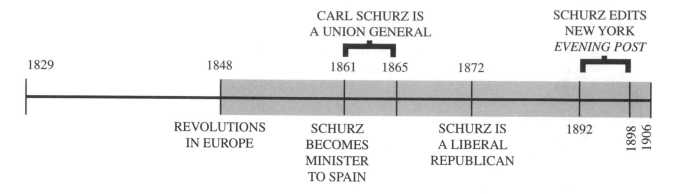

QUESTIONS FOR RESEARCH

1. What is the Pulitzer Prize? Does it reflect, in any way, the principles held by Carl Schurz?

2. What did the word *kindergarten* mean in translation? Were there other German ideas in education and agriculture that were brought to America by the new immigrants?

3. What is the principle behind the civil service system? Has it served to better American governing processes?

NATIONAL STANDARDS CORRELATIONS

NCSS Ic: (Culture) Explain and give examples of how language, literature, the arts, architecture, other artifacts, traditions, beliefs, values, and behaviors contribute to the development and transmission of cultures.

NSH Era 6, Standard 2: Massive immigration after 1870 and how new social patterns, conflicts, and ideas of national unity developed amid growing cultural diversity

WEBSITES

http://www.pulitzer.org/
"The Pulitzer Prizes: 2005," The Pulitzer Prizes

http://www.digitalhistory.uh.edu/database/subtitles.cfm?titleID=23
"Guided Readings: The Struggle for Public School," Digital History

http://www.digitalhistory.uh.edu/database/article_display.cfm?HHID=145
"Civil Service Reform," Digital History

http://usinfo.state.gov/usa/infousa/facts/democrac/28.htm
"Backgrounder on the Pendleton Act," International Information Programs, U.S. Department of State

Name: _____ Date: _____

Carl Schurz (cont.)

HISTORICAL FACTS

1. Carl Schurz was born in _____, coming to the United States after the 1848 German revolutions failed.

2. Schurz's wife introduced the _____ idea to this country.

3. In 1860, he worked diligently on _____'s presidential campaign and was rewarded with an appointment as the U.S. Minister to Spain.

4. He was made a _____ in the Union Army.

5. Schurz became the editor of the very powerful German-language newspaper, the *Westliche Post* of _____.

6. _____ was employed by Schurz at this time.

7. Schurz led most of the Illinois and Missouri German-Americans into the _____ _____ of 1872.

8. He backed _____ against Ulysses S. Grant, and of course, backed the wrong person; the way back into national politics was difficult.

9. He became a Missouri senator and pushed for the election of _____ in 1876.

10. He eventually became _____.

11. He pushed for the introduction of the _____ system, which helped eliminate some parts of the spoils system operating at that time.

12. He became the editor of the _____ in 1892.

Alfred Thayer Mahan

1840–1914

Alfred Thayer Mahan

It is doubtful that the ordinary American citizen today would be able to identify Alfred Thayer Mahan. Yet Mahan had an enormous effect on America during his lifetime, and the reaction of the United States to his doctrines has echoed down to the present day.

Mahan was born in 1840 in West Point, New York. He attended private school in Hagerstown, Maryland, and after several years at Columbia College, he won an appointment to the United States Naval Academy. At Annapolis, Mahan did quite well and graduated with second honors in 1859. From 1859 to 1861, Mahan was ordered to service aboard the *Congress*, which was sent on a cruise to Brazil.

During the Civil War, Mahan was appointed to the rank of lieutenant, and he served on blockade duty along the east coast. He served on Admiral Dahlgren's staff in the last year of the war. Following the war, he was assigned to the *Iroquois*, which had a long tour of duty in the Far East. In the years between 1867 and 1885, Mahan did a considerable amount of writing, commencing with a Civil War history entitled *The Gulf and Inland Waters*. These literary efforts sharpened his style and his ability to present naval tactics in an understandable way.

The turning point in his life, and in American naval history, came with his appointment as lecturer at the War College at Newport. Here, in 1886, Mahan began a series of lectures that were to have a great effect on the world. In 1890, the lectures were published under the title *The Influence of Sea Power Upon History, 1660–1783*. The lectures concentrated on the close interrelationship of sea power and politics.

Mahan continued his "sea power" lectures after 1890, publishing them as he produced them. Their impact on international development was tremendous. Theodore Roosevelt correctly wrote: "I am greatly in error if it does not become a classic." British statesmen read them, not only as vindication of their empire, but as gospel that should be followed. Kaiser Wilhelm II of Germany wrote of "devouring" the writings of Mahan, something he must have done, because he immediately began to build a navy.

At the moment of Mahan's lectures, most European nations were engaged in colonial exploitation. Mahan argued that to have a navy, a nation must have colonies; to have colonies, a nation must have a navy. In application to the United States, Mahan's theories were immediately seen in various colonial additions. Islands in the Pacific, the Philippines, and eventually the Panama Canal were all related to the Mahan thesis. In relation to the Canal, Mahan might have argued the following: to have an active two-ocean navy, a nation must have a canal in Panama; to have a canal in Panama, a nation must protect it with a strong navy.

Virtually every nation with dreams of an empire was affected by Mahan's books. As previously mentioned, the British and the Germans followed the Mahan argument; so did the Japanese, who quickly translated Mahan's books into their language.

It is difficult to imagine that Mahan could have written anything more important than his "sea power" lectures. He did write a good deal of history, though, including books on Admiral Nelson, Admiral Farragut, naval strategy in the American Revolution, and sea power in the War of 1812.

Mahan lived long enough to see one application of his theories on sea power—he was still alive at the beginning of World War I in 1914. But before the end of that year, he died.

Alfred Thayer Mahan (cont.)

One last thought! It is possible to translate Mahan's sea power into terms of the present. A nation, to be powerful, must have air power, but to have air power, it must have bases. To have bases for a nation's air power, that nation must also have air power to protect those bases.

TIME LINE

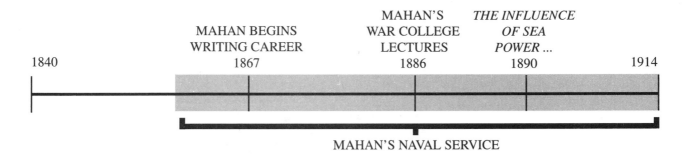

MAHAN'S NAVAL SERVICE

QUESTIONS FOR RESEARCH

1. Research the great naval race that began after 1900. Which nations were involved in that naval race?

2. Mahan's writings were partially responsible for the acquisition by the U.S. of the Philippines, Puerto Rico, Guam, and other island possessions. When the United States got into the Philippines, the nation became an Asiatic power. In what conflicts has the United States been involved that are traceable to being an Asiatic power?

3. In what way is the Panama Canal a direct result of Mahan's thinking?

NATIONAL STANDARDS CORRELATIONS

NCSS VIf: (Power, Authority, & Governance) Explain conditions, actions, and motivations that contribute to conflict and cooperation within and among nations.
NSH Era 6, Standard 4: Federal Indian policy and United States foreign policy after the Civil War

WEBSITES

http//memory.log.gov/cgi-bin/query/r?ammem/ncps:@field(DOCID+@lit(ABK2934-0066-126))::
"The United States Looking Outward. [*The Atlantic Monthly*/Volume 66, Issue 398, December 1890],"
The Library of Congress

http://www.historicaltextarchive.com/sections.php?op=viewarticle&artid=332
"Acquisition of the Panama Canal," Donald J. Mabry/The Historical Text Archive

http://memory.loc.gov/cig-bin/query/r?ammem/ncps:@field(DOCID+@lit(ABD2934-0072-75))::(
"The Isthmus of Sea Power. [*The Atlantic Monthly*/Volume 72, Issue 432, October 1893]," The Library of Congress

Name: _____   Date: _____

Alfred Thayer Mahan (cont.)

HISTORICAL FACTS

1. Mahan was born in 1840 in _____.

2. He graduated from the _____ with honors in 1859.

3. Mahan was ordered to service aboard the _____, which was sent on a cruise to Brazil.

4. During the _____, Mahan served on blockade duty along the east coast.

5. He did a considerable amount of writing, commencing with a history of the war entitled

   _____.

6. He became a lecturer at the _____ at Newport; these lectures were to have a great effect on the world.

7. In 1890, the lectures were published under the title _____

   _____.

8. He continued his "sea power" lectures after _____, publishing them as he produced them.

9. Kaiser Wilhelm II of Germany wrote of "devouring" the writings of Mahan. He immediately began building a _____.

10. Mahan said to have a navy, a nation must have _____; and to have _____, a nation must have a navy.

11. Every nation with dreams of an _____ was affected by Mahan's book.

12. The _____ quickly translated Mahan's books into their language.

Booker T. Washington

1856–1915

In the years following the Civil War, education for African-Americans in the South had a fitful beginning. It was forced to operate under many handicaps, such as financial problems and racial bias. During the Reconstruction Period, the only support for African-American educational institutions in the South came from northern philanthropists. In 1868, Hampton Institute was founded, and 1881 saw the founding of Tuskegee Institute.

Both of these institutes primarily stressed education of a vocational nature, because attitudes of the time indicated that this was the best direction for African-Americans to go.

One of the foremost African-American educators of the period was Booker Taliaferro Washington. Born into slavery in Virginia, young Washington was at least nine years of age before

Booker T. Washington dines with Theodore Roosevelt at the White House.

he was fully free. In West Virginia, where his family had moved, Washington attended a type of mission school, although it was his own drive and intelligence that urged him to succeed in conquering illiteracy. He entered Hampton Institute in 1872 and, while at that institution, learned to be a bricklayer. Later, he went into teaching at a small school at Malden, West Virginia, and from there he found his way back to Hampton Institute as an instructor.

His personality was such that when he was called upon to form a new school in Alabama, he leapt at the chance with great fervor. His enthusiasm was met with crushing disappointment, however. When he arrived at Tuskegee, he found his "new school" to be nothing more than a shed. Determined to succeed, he proceeded to raise money—mainly by going on speaking tours throughout the North. He soon had buildings at Tuskegee; but as president of the institution, he took the attitude that African-Americans could best advance in society by being efficient and able workers. Tuskegee, therefore, became heavy in vocational subjects—a tendency for which Washington is sometimes criticized by African-Americans in later years. It must be pointed out, however, that new state normal schools throughout the land were going in the same direction—towards a heavy emphasis on vocationalism.

While Washington continued to advocate a kind of partnership between African-Americans and whites in the South, with the African-Americans taking a more submissive role, other African-American leaders proceeded to form the National Association for the Advancement of Colored People. This group espoused a more vigorous policy of obtaining equality than did those who followed Washington.

Washington's Tuskegee Institute continued to grow, however, and Washington himself remained as the principal African-American spokesman in America. During President Theodore Roosevelt's administration, Washington was invited to the White House. There was hope on the part of many African-Americans that the meeting between the two men would lead to gains for their race.

Unfortunately, such was not the case. Just before his death, Washington bitterly complained that African-Americans had been promised a "new freedom," but, "On the contrary," Washington concluded, "we are given a stone instead of a loaf of bread."

Booker T. Washington (cont.)

TIME LINE

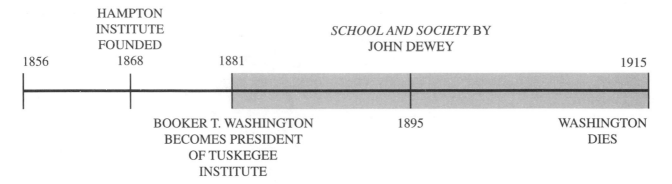

QUESTIONS FOR RESEARCH

1. What is the attitude of present-day African-American leaders towards the image of Booker T. Washington? Research Washington's Atlanta Compromise.

2. In advocating vocationalism, was B.T. Washington really too much out of line with John Dewey's attitudes, as expressed in his important *School and Society?*

3. What is the status of Tuskegee Institute today? Is it highly regarded among African-American institutions in the South?

NATIONAL STANDARDS CORRELATIONS

NCSS Vc: (Individuals, Groups, & Institutions) Describe various forms institutions take and the interactions of people with institutions.
NSH Era 5, Standard 3: How various Reconstruction plans succeeded or failed.

WEBSITES

http://memory.loc.gov/ammem/aaohtml/exhibit/aopart6.html
"The Booker T. Washington Era," The Library of Congress

http://www.americaslibrary.gov/cgi-bin/page.cgi/jb/progress/btwash_1
"Booker T. Washington Delivered the 'Atlanta Compromise' September 18, 1895," The Library of Congress

http://www.cr.nps.gov/museum/exhibits/tuskegee/
"Legends of Tuskegee," National Park Service

Name: _____ Date: _____

Booker T. Washington (cont.)

HISTORICAL FACTS

1. During the Reconstruction Period, the only support for African-American education at institutions in the South came from _____.

2. In 1868, _____ was founded, and 1881 saw the founding of _____.

3. One of the foremost African-American educators of the period was _____ _____.

4. Born as a slave, Washington was at least nine before he was fully free. He used his own drive and intelligence to urge himself to succeed in conquering illiteracy. He entered _____ _____ in 1872, and while at the institute learned to be a _____.

5. Later, though, he went to teach at a small school at _____, and from there he found his way back to Hampton Institute as an instructor.

6. Washington was asked to form a new school in _____.

7. He started with nothing more than just a shed, but after speaking tours throughout the North, he soon had buildings at _____.

8. The school became heavy in _____ subjects, a tendency for which Washington is sometimes criticized by African-Americans in later years.

9. Other African-American leaders formed the _____ _____. This group espoused a more vigorous policy of obtaining equality than did those who followed Washington.

10. Washington's Tuskegee Institute continued to grow, however, and Washington himself remained the principal African-American _____ in America.

11. During President _____'s administration, Washington was invited to the White House.

12. African-Americans had been promised a "new freedom" but, "On the contrary," Washington concluded, "we are given a _____ instead of a _____."

83

Terence Powderly

1849–1924

Terence Powderly

Until 1860, the laboring class of the United States had little need for the protection of labor unions. But the Civil War brought great industrialization to the country, and the surge of immigration to the United States after the war allowed for cheap labor and the institution of labor abuses. The natural reaction of the American worker was to organize for his own protection.

Terence Powderly was born in 1849, shortly before the need for, and the growth of, American labor unions. His father and mother were Irish immigrants who settled in Carbondale, Pennsylvania, where Powderly's father worked for a coal company. Young Powderly worked as a machinist from 1869 to 1877. During the early part of this period, he joined the Machinists' and Blacksmiths' Union, and he soon became a leader in that organization.

By this time, one of the growing forces in the country was a semi-secret labor union called the Knights of Labor. This union, following the fashion of the times as expressed in the growing number of fraternal organizations, had a secret ritual as part of its organizational routine. Unfortunately for the union, this secrecy denied a large part of the American working class access to membership. This was particularly true of American Catholics who were involved in much of the unskilled labor of the country and whose religion forbade involvement in such rituals.

Powderly joined the Knights of Labor in Philadelphia and soon worked his way up in the structure of the union. In 1878, he pushed through changes in the Knights of Labor constitution, the most important of which was a preamble based on the concept of industrial brotherhood.

In 1879, he was chosen Grand Master Workman (later General Master Workman), an office he held until 1893. During that same period, he served as the mayor of Scranton, Pennsylvania, for three consecutive terms.

Powderly's effect on the Knights of Labor was a significant one. He was much more idealistic than aggressive, and he saw the union as having educational purposes. By the dissemination of information, he hoped to see the abuses of labor corrected by mass opposition on the part of laboring men. He did not like strikes. He pushed the concept of cooperatives, and at the same time, he argued that immediate goals such as higher wages and shorter hours were secondary to the abolition of the wage system.

During the 1880s, the Knights of Labor was wrongly associated by the public with the famous Haymarket Riot in Chicago. The general result was a decline in the appeal of the union. Nevertheless, Powderly acceded to the growing influence of the American Federation of Labor without too much opposition, and he even went so far as to agree in principle with the organization of a political party based on a unity between laboring and farming interests.

But, as the Knights declined, so did Powderly's influence. In 1894, he took and passed an examination for the bar and became a practicing lawyer. By now he had grown more and more interested in the cause of the National Republican Party which, in the 1890s, was perhaps the more liberal of the two major parties. His work for the Republican ticket brought him an appointment as commissioner-general of immigration, and in that position, he implemented rules to keep physically and mentally handicapped people from entering the country.

84

Terence Powderly (cont.)

Powderly did some writing in his life, and his notions about the labor movement can be found in the various publications of the Knights of Labor. Powderly died in 1924 at the age of seventy-five. He is generally remembered as the first of America's great union leaders.

TIME LINE

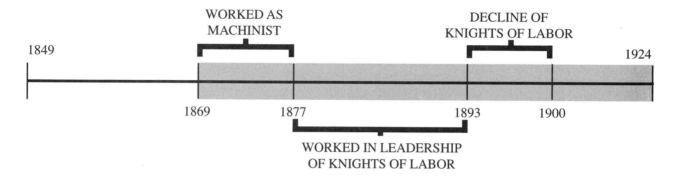

QUESTIONS FOR RESEARCH

1. Some labor historians would not describe Terence V. Powderly as a good labor leader. Why? In your own estimation, did Powderly fit the times in which he lived?

2. In general, what were the aims of laboring people in the period following the Civil War? What was the cooperative idea?

3. In the period following the Civil War, did American big business regard the laboring class as having any rights at all? What did the laboring person fall back on if he lost his job, was injured, or became ill? Did he have unemployment insurance, social security, or any safeguards?

NATIONAL STANDARDS CORRELATIONS

NCSS Vg: (Individuals, Groups, & Institutions) Apply knowledge of how groups and institutions work to meet individual needs and promote the common good.
NSH Era 6, Standard 3: The rise of the American labor movement and how political issues reflected social and economic changes

WEBSITES

http://historymatters.gmu.edu/d/96/
"'A Healthy Public Opinion': Terence V. Powderly Distances the Knights of Labor From the Haymarket Martyrs," American Social History Productions, Inc.

http://memory.loc.gov/ammem/award98/ichihtml/hayhome.html
"Chicago Anarchists on Trial: Evidence from the Haymarket Affair, 1886–1887," The Library of Congress

Terence Powderly (cont.)

HISTORICAL FACTS

1. Until _____, the laboring class of the United States had little need for the protection

   of labor unions.

2. The Civil War brought great _____ and a surge of

   _____ to the country.

3. The American worker organized for his own _____.

4. Terence Powderly worked as a _____ from 1869 to 1877.

5. During this period, he joined the Machinists' and Blacksmiths' _____, where

   he soon became a leader in that organization.

6. Also by this time, the semi-secret union called _____ was

   gaining strength and momentum.

7. Powderly joined this ritualistic union in _____ and worked his way up in

   the structure.

8. American Catholics were involved in much of the _____ labor of the country,

   but their religion forbade them from involvement in the rituals of this union.

9. In 1879, he was chosen _____, an office he

   held until 1893.

10. He served as mayor of _____ for three consecutive terms.

11. Powderly did not like _____. He pushed the idea of cooperatives.

12. The Knights of Labor were wrongfully linked to the Haymarket Riot in _____.

13. The Knights declined, the _____ gained power,

    and Powderly's influence waned.

Samuel Gompers

1850–1924

Samuel Gompers

Although Samuel Gompers was born in London in 1850, his parents were of Dutch and Jewish extraction. When he was thirteen years of age, he came to the United States. Only one year later, he became the first registered member of the Cigarmakers' International Union—an organization that he eventually made into one of the most effective labor organizations in the country.

It is interesting to note how cigars were made in the nineteenth century. All cigars were made by hand and were usually put together in small and dingy "factories." In fact, many cigar stores actually had a cigar maker working in their display windows, in full sight of customers who were passing by. The leaves were rolled by hand and, in most cases, simply stuck together by what one manufacturer called "sweat and spit." Tuberculosis was common among cigar makers, and it can be assumed that the disease was transmitted to cigar users.

When Gompers was twenty-six years old, he led the movement to establish a new labor organization called the American Federation of Labor. There had been previous national labor unions—the Knights of Labor, for instance—but these had all failed. The A.F. of L. was a craft union; that is, it was composed of various member unions of skilled workers throughout the country. In that time, as well as now, the skilled worker category included carpenters, plumbers, etc.

By 1893, the time of the depression of the 1890s, the Federation could count a membership of 265,000. With the exception of the United Mine Workers of America, which developed at the turn of the century, the A.F. of L. failed to organize in the oil and steel industries. Still, growth in membership continued to be phenomenal, and in 1919, when Gompers was still president of the organization, the number of dues-paying members had reached 4.1 million.

Gompers always insisted that labor should not commit itself to either of the two major political parties. He never wanted a labor party (such as had been created in England), but he saw value in playing one party against another for general gains. Such a policy caused some of the more radical labor leaders to look upon Gompers as unaggressive, and from time to time there were attempts to unseat the old man. Yet, even today, it is not possible to say that Gompers was wrong in his notion of handling labor's political aims.

Gompers campaigned hard against anti-strike laws, for he considered the strike to be labor's only weapon. He also worked hard to establish laws to regulate the conditions under which women and children worked, although he did not live to see the nation rid of child labor.

Gompers died in 1924, and the leadership of the A.F. of L. passed into the hands of William Green. Later, in the 1930s, a rival national union, the Committee for Industrial Organization (C.I.O.) organized workers in iron and steel, the automobile plants, and other industries. Still later, the two great national unions were merged into the A.F.L.-C.I.O.

Samuel Gompers (cont.)

TIME LINE

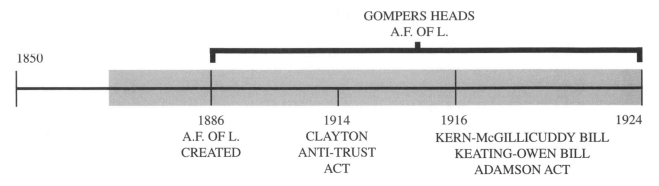

GOMPERS HEADS
A.F. OF L.

1850

1886
A.F. OF L.
CREATED

1914
CLAYTON
ANTI-TRUST
ACT

1916
KERN-McGILLICUDDY BILL
KEATING-OWEN BILL
ADAMSON ACT

1924

QUESTIONS FOR RESEARCH

1. Locate any photographs of child labor as it existed at the turn of the century.

2. In regard to Gompers' policy of switching support for political parties, trace labor's support of presidential candidates from 1900 to present.

3. In the 1930s, a labor union official, not mentioned in this piece, undertook to organize the iron and steel workers and the automobile industry. What was his name, and what troubles did the organizers have in establishing the C.I.O.?

NATIONAL STANDARDS CORRELATIONS

NCSS Vg: (Individuals, Groups, & Insitutitons) Apply knowledge of how groups and institutions work to meet individual needs and promote the common good.
NSH Era 6: Standard 3: The rise of the American labor movement and how political issues reflected social and economic changes

WEBSITES

http://www.history.umd.edu/Gompers/index.htm
"The Samuel Gompers Papers," Sponsored by the University of Maryland College Park, the National Historical Publications and Records Commission, the National Endowment for the Humanities, and the AFL-CIO

http://www.aflcio.org/aboutus/history/history/gompers.cfm
"Samuel Gompers (1850–1924)," AFL-CIO

http://www.pbs.org/newshour/bb/election/july-dec99/historians_10-12.html
"Labor's Historical Impact, October 12, 1999," MacNeil/Lehrer Productions

Name: _____ Date: _____

Samuel Gompers (cont.)

HISTORICAL FACTS

1. Although Sam Gompers was born in _____ in _____, his parents were of Dutch and Jewish extraction.

2. When he was _____ years of age he came to the United States.

3. He became the first registered member of the _____.

4. Tobacco leaves were rolled by hand and, in most cases, simply stuck together by what one manufacturer called " _____ and _____."

5. _____ was common among cigar makers, and it can be assumed that the disease was transmitted to cigar users.

6. When Gompers was twenty-six years old, he led the movement to establish a new labor organization called the _____.

7. By 1893, the time of the depression of the 1890s, the Federation could count a membership of _____.

8. In 1919, when Gompers was still president of the organization, the number of dues-paying members had reached _____ million.

9. Gompers insisted that labor should be committed to _____ political party.

10. Gompers campaigned hard against _____ laws, for he considered the _____ to be labor's only weapon.

11. He also worked hard to establish laws to regulate the conditions under which _____ and _____ worked.

12. Gompers died in _____. Later, the two great national unions were merged into the _____.

Charles William Eliot

1834–1926

Charles William Eliot was one of the greatest educational leaders in the history of the United States. He was born to New England Yankee stock in 1834. His entire life seems to have been associated with Harvard College. Charles's father was the treasurer and historian of the college, and Charles himself was enrolled in the institution in 1849—at only fifteen years of age. There he came under the influence of such men as Benjamin Pierce, Louis Agassiz, Asa Gray, and Josiah Parsons Cooke.

Charles William Eliot

Four years after his graduation, Charles became a professor at Harvard. As one of the youngest professors in the history of the institution, Eliot introduced laboratory exercises, elective instruction, and written examinations.

In 1865, and later in 1867, Eliot made first-hand observations of education in Europe. Shortly after his return, he wrote an interesting article on his experiences for *Atlantic Monthly*, and this, plus his growing reputation, caused his appointment to the presidency of Harvard.

The changes brought about by Eliot at Harvard were not only revolutionary at that college but were powerful in terms of having a national impact. During his lifetime, the school quadrupled in student size, and it added graduate schools in arts and sciences, applied science and business, and courses in such wide and diverse areas as architecture and forestry.

Eliot also brought women members into the faculty and recruited leading professors in foreign countries for the Harvard staff. He developed "exchange professorships," introduced the notion of sabbatical leaves, and developed a liberal system of retirement allowances. All three of these latter reforms were so far ahead of the situation in the rest of the nation that some colleges still did not have them as late as 1930.

Eliot also introduced the notion of allowing students to carry more courses during a term and pushed a plan to allow the medical college to grant the M.D. after three years of study.

Eliot's writings were so voluminous that one wonders how he did it all. He wrote enough to fill at least eight volumes, as well as the *Reports of the President of Harvard College*. These last are still considered prime reading in the study of higher education.

Besides all of this, Eliot edited the *Harvard Classics*. He had once made a remark that a man could obtain a liberal education by reading only fifteen minutes a day. Being challenged on that statement, he undertook to prepare a range of reading that could prove his point. So widely was Eliot respected in the United States that the *Harvard Classics* became best-selling publications, to be found in the homes of many American families.

It could be said that higher education in America from 1850 to 1930 was marked by the dominance of imposing and effective college presidents. Among these would be such men as Angell, McCosh, Hopkins, and Eliot himself. They were important, not only because of the changes they made in American colleges and universities, but for a number of other reasons as well. They created a distinctive system of higher education that was truly American. Most of all, however, by their imposing intellectuality, they developed among their students a profound respect for the world of learning.

Charles William Eliot (cont.)

TIME LINE

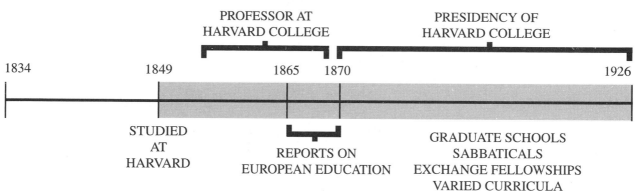

QUESTIONS FOR RESEARCH

1. Trace the early years of Harvard College. What courses were offered? Who could attend?

2. Do you have any of Eliot's *Harvard Classics* in your library? What does Eliot seem to stress in them?

3. What is a "liberal arts" education, and how does it differ from a vocational education?

NATIONAL STANDARDS CORRELATIONS

<u>**NCSS Vg:**</u> (Individuals, Groups, & Institutions) Apply knowledge of how groups and institutions work to meet individual needs and promote the common good.
<u>**NSH Era 7, Standard 3:**</u> How the United States changed from the end of World War I to the eve of the Great Depression

WEBSITES

http://www.ed.gov/pubs/VoEd/Chapter2/Part3.html
"The Quality of Vocational Education, June 1998," U.S. Department of Education

http://www.iseek.org/sv/2005.jsp#definition
"The Role of Liberal Arts in Your Future," ISEEK, the Internet System for Education and Employment Knowledge

http://www.harvardmagazine.com/on-line/110177.html
"Eliot's Elect: The Harvard Classics, 1910," Harvard Magazine, Inc.

Name: _____   Date: _____

Charles William Eliot (cont.)

HISTORICAL FACTS

1. Charles William Eliot was one of the greatest _____ leaders

    in the history of the United States.

2. His entire life seems to have been associated with _____.

3. He was enrolled in the college at age 15; four years after graduation, he became a _____

    at the institution.

4. Eliot became _____ of Harvard College.

5. During his tenure at Harvard College, the student population quadrupled and he added several

    _____ schools.

6. He also brought _____ members into the faculty.

7. Eliot's writings filled eight volumes, as well as the _____.

8. He also edited the _____.

9. Eliot once made a remark that a man could obtain a liberal education by reading only

    _____ minutes a day.

10. The *Harvard Classics* became best-selling publications and could be found in the _____

    of many American families.

11. Higher education in America from _____ to _____ was marked by the

    dominance of imposing and effective college presidents.

12. These presidents developed among their students a profound respect for _____

    _____.

13. Eliot died in 1926 at age _____.

Oliver Wendell Holmes, Jr.

1841–1935

Oliver Wendell Holmes, Jr., was born on March 8, 1841, just after the inauguration of William Henry Harrison as President of the United States. His lifetime spanned the administrations of Tyler, Polk, Taylor, Fillmore, Pierce, Buchanan, Lincoln, Johnson, Grant, Hayes, Garfield, Arthur, Cleveland, Harrison, Cleveland (second term), McKinley, Roosevelt, Taft, Wilson, Harding, Coolidge, and Herbert Hoover. He lived until 1935, which was the third year of the first term of Franklin Delano Roosevelt.

Oliver Wendell Holmes, Jr.

Oliver's father was, of course, the famous poet, raconteur, and physician—Oliver Wendell Holmes. The fame of the elder man plagued his son for years, for Oliver's personality was entirely unlike that of his father. Much more retiring, he wanted to be known for his own achievements, rather than those of his father.

Oliver Wendell Holmes, Jr., was twenty years old when the Civil War broke out. He enlisted almost immediately, quickly became an officer, and was wounded three times during the conflict. During one of his long convalescences, his father wrote an account for publication of his own pilgrimage to the bedside of his son. Young Oliver did not appreciate this at all, and there was a temporary estrangement between them.

After the war, Holmes entered the Harvard Law School. He quickly became the co-editor of the *American Law Review*, and in 1881 wrote a most influential book entitled *The Common Law*.

Shortly thereafter, he was appointed to the Supreme Judicial Court of Massachusetts and became the Chief Justice of that state in 1899. During this period, his statements on law, as well as his decisions, earned him the reputation as a "progressive." It truly did seem, for a while, that he would reach no higher in life.

In 1902, however, Theodore Roosevelt appointed Holmes to the Supreme Court—all the while hoping that the new appointee would be a "Roosevelt man." Of course Holmes wasn't, and the new justice's pithy and sensible statements on legal decisions soon led the press to refer to him as "the great dissenter."

Oliver Wendell Holmes, Jr., never became the Chief Justice of the Supreme Court. It is possible that he could have won the appointment; it is also possible that he didn't want it. At any rate, he established a reputation for justice and honor throughout his years of service on the Supreme Court.

As a court justice, Holmes tutored some of the great legal minds of America; they were his legal assistants. Since he and his wife had never had any children of their own, he liked to call his assistants his "boys."

Holmes' decisions served to bring about much social change, and they generally followed his own maxim: "The life of the law has not been logic; it has been experience."

93

Oliver Wendell Holmes, Jr. (cont.)

TIME LINE

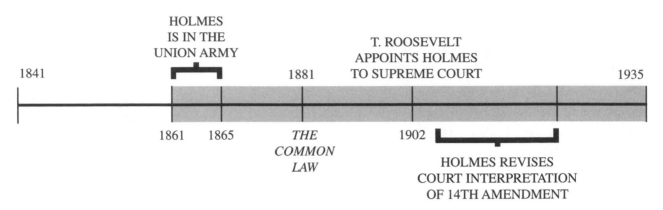

QUESTIONS FOR RESEARCH

1. One of the great human dramas in American history was the relationship between the two famous Holmeses. After researching the two men, what do you think Oliver Wendell Holmes, Jr.'s, major complaint was about his father?

2. Use biographies or writings about Holmes to create a list of great lawyers who worked with "the great dissenter."

3. Holmes liked to write his decisions in an understandable manner. One of his most quoted statements concerns the limits of freedom of speech. Find Holmes' comment. By the way, Holmes met Abraham Lincoln. Where and under what circumstances?

NATIONAL STANDARDS CORRELATIONS

NCSS IIf: (Time, Continuity, & Change) Use knowledge of facts and concepts drawn from history, along with methods of historical inquiry, to inform decision-making about and action-taking on public issues.

NSH Era 7, Standard 1: How Progressives and others addressed problems of industrial capitalism, urbanization, and political corruption

WEBSITES

http://www.supremecourthistory.org/02_history/subs_timeline/images_associates/049.html
"Oliver Wendell Holmes, Jr.," The Supreme Court Historical Society

http://odur.let.rug.nl/~usa/B/oliver/oliverxx.htm
"Justice Oliver Wendell Holmes, Jr. (1841–1935)," Department of Humanities Computing, University of Groningen, The Netherlands

http://www.historycentral.com/bio/rec/OliverWendellHolmes.html
"Oliver Wendell Holmes," MultiEducator, Inc.

Name: _____ Date: _____

Oliver Wendell Holmes, Jr. (cont.)

HISTORICAL FACTS

1. Oliver Wendell Holmes, Jr., was born on _____.

2. His lifetime spanned the administrations of _____ different presidents and into the third year of Franklin Delano Roosevelt's first term.

3. Oliver's father was the famous _____ and _____ Oliver Wendell Holmes.

4. Oliver Wendell Holmes, Jr., was twenty years old when the _____ broke out.

5. Wounded _____ times in the war, he was upset that his father wrote an account for publication of his own pilgrimage to the bedside of his son.

6. After the war, Holmes entered the _____ School.

7. He quickly became the co-editor of the _____, and in 1881 wrote a most influential book entitled _____.

8. He was appointed to the Supreme Judicial Court of Massachusetts and became the _____ of that state in 1899.

9. In 1902, Theodore Roosevelt appointed Holmes to the _____.

10. Oliver Wendell Holmes never became _____ of the Supreme Court.

11. He established a reputation for _____ and _____ throughout his years of service on the Supreme Court.

12. As a court justice, Holmes tutored some _____ of America.

George W. Norris

1861–1944

George William Norris was born in Ohio in 1861. He was one of the greatest statesmen in the history of American public life. His hallmark was independence. As a congressman, he never hesitated to put his own political party far behind the national interest—even if it meant censure from his colleagues.

George W. Norris

He studied at Valparaiso University in Indiana. When he was twenty-four, he moved to Nebraska. Norris was first elected to the U.S. House of Representatives in 1902—during the high point of the Progressive Movement. In 1910, when House insurgents attempted to challenge the power of Speaker of the House Joseph Cannon, Norris led the campaign. Despite every attempt by the wily Cannon to oppose the changes in House rules, Norris won the day, thus paving the way for fundamental reforms.

In 1912, Norris was elected a United States senator from Nebraska. In 1917, when the issue of America's entrance into the war was at hand, Norris led a brief but futile fight to keep the country out of Europe's troubles. After the war, Norris opposed U.S. entry into the League of Nations, thinking that American participation here would lead the nation into more wars.

Norris's great interest was in the extension of publicly owned utilities. The great dam, Muscle Shoals, in Alabama, had been built during the war to provide cheap electricity for farmers. During the years of the Harding-Coolidge administration (1921–1925), there were numerous attempts by private enterprises to obtain control of the dam. Norris opposed them all, even blocking the lease of the project to Henry Ford for $5 million.

What Norris really wanted was to incorporate the Muscle Shoals Dam into a larger complex of proposed dams on the Tennessee River. Opposed by his own Republican Party, Norris led the fight in 1933 to establish the Tennessee Valley Authority.

In time, the TVA built thirty dams on the Tennessee and its tributaries. Nine of the high dams created huge man-made lakes, such as Kentucky Lake, and provided electrical power to a poor region. Parks were created, trees and grass were planted over eroded areas, soil fertility was restored—these, and a new way of life, were by-products of TVA.

It is somewhat important to understand that Norris did not come from Appalachia. He came from Nebraska—some distance away. As a salute to his efforts, one of the dams on the Tennessee was named after him.

Norris also helped to enact the Twentieth Amendment to the Constitution. In the late 1930s, Norris realized the dangers of the spread of fascism in Europe, and gave his support for aid to Great Britain. It may have been this factor that led to his defeat for the Senate in 1942.

George W. Norris (cont.)

TIME LINE

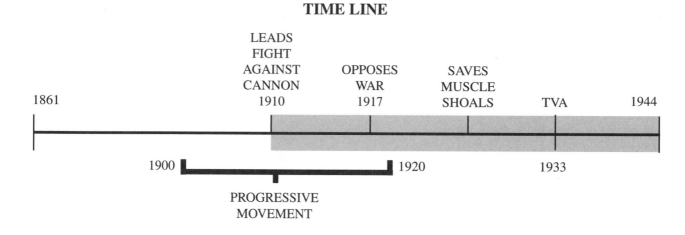

QUESTIONS FOR RESEARCH

1. What does the Twentieth Amendment to the Constitution state?

2. Research the Tennessee Valley Authority, sometimes called one of the Seven Wonders of the Modern World. Chattanooga is a city that was affected by the TVA. Identify what changes have occurred in that city since 1933.

3. There was a time in Norris's career when he ran as an "Independent." What does that mean?

NATIONAL STANDARDS CORRELATIONS

NCSS IIIi: (People, Places, & Environments) Describe ways that historical events have been influenced by, and have influenced, physical and human geographic factors in local, regional, national, and global settings.

NSH Era 7, Standard 1: How Progressives and others addressed problems of industrial capitalism, urbanization, and political corruption

WEBSITES

http://newdeal.feri.org/tva/
"TVA: Electricity for All," New Deal Network

http://www.tva.gov/abouttva/history.htm
"From a New Deal to a New Century," Tennessee Valley Authority

http://bioguide.congress.gov/scripts/biodisplay.pl?index=N000139
"Norris, George William (1861–1944)," Biographical Directory of the United States Congress

Name: _____   Date: _____

George W. Norris (cont.)

HISTORICAL FACTS

1. Norris was born in Ohio in _____.

2. George William Norris was one of the greatest _____ in the

   history of American public life.

3. His hallmark was _____.

4. He studied at _____ in Indiana. When he was twenty-

   four, he moved to Nebraska.

5. Norris was first elected to the _____ in 1902.

6. This was during the high point of the _____ Movement.

7. In 1912, Norris was elected a _____ from Nebraska.

8. Norris opposed U.S. entry into the _____, thinking that it

   would lead the nation into more wars.

9. Norris's great interest was in the extension of publicly owned _____.

10. The great dam, _____, in Alabama had been built during the

    war to provide cheap electricity for farmers.

11. Norris blocked the leasing of this dam by Henry Ford for $ _____.

12. Norris led the fight in 1933 to establish the _____.

13. In time, the TVA built _____ dams on the Tennessee and its tributaries.

14. Norris also helped to enact the _____ Amendment to the Constitution.

15. In order to stop the spread of _____ in Europe, Norris supported giving

    aid to Great Britain.

John J. Pershing

1860–1948

John J. Pershing

John Joseph Pershing was born in 1860, in Linn County, Missouri, and spent his boyhood in Laclede, Missouri. His father was a railroad worker who spurred young Pershing towards a solid education. At the age of seventeen, Pershing began a short teaching career at an African-American school, but soon left that job to enter the Kirksville Normal School. While in this institution, he passed the examination for the U.S. Military Academy, a school from which he graduated in 1886.

Pershing's military career was wide and varied. He took part in campaigns against the Apache and the Sioux, and later he was an instructor at West Point. During the Spanish-American War, he was an officer with the 10th Cavalry, a unit of African-American soldiers. Due to this and later associations with African-American troops, he was known throughout the service as "Black Jack."

During the insurrection in the Philippines, Pershing campaigned against the fierce Moro tribesmen. In 1904, he became an observer in the Russo-Japanese War. In 1906, because of an impression made upon President Theodore Roosevelt, Pershing was promoted to the rank of brigadier general. In 1916, he was placed in command of an army sent to capture the Mexican bandit Pancho Villa.

Pershing's private life was one long episode of tragedy, and there were times when he felt seriously inclined to leave the military service. Yet, in 1917, when the United States entered World War I, he was quickly chosen to lead the rapidly forming American divisions in Europe. President Wilson's decision to entrust Pershing with the command of the American Expeditionary Force was probably based upon two reasons. First of all, Pershing had become well-known during the 1916 campaign in Mexico. Second, through some error in record keeping, it was thought that Pershing spoke French.

Almost immediately, Pershing caught the fancy of the American public. Shortly after arriving in France, he laid a wreath at the tomb of the Marquis de Lafayette. One of his aides gave a short speech during these ceremonies, at which time the famous phrase, "Lafayette, we are here" was uttered. Though Pershing never made the statement, the French public, as well as the American people, associated the tactful phrase with Pershing himself.

Pershings's contributions to the Allied war effort were many. He was a strict disciplinarian, and he demanded that American troops be maintained within the organization of the American Expeditionary Force. Though this irritated other Allied generals, in the end Pershing's notions were right. His insistence upon rifle and attack tactics also paid off, in the sense that American troops did well on the field of battle, despite an obvious lack of experience in other respects.

Perhaps more than anything else, it was Pershing who nurtured and maintained a bright young officer corps that, some twenty years later, was of invaluable service to the nation. Two of these men were George Catlett Marshall and Douglas MacArthur.

John J. Pershing (cont.)

TIME LINE

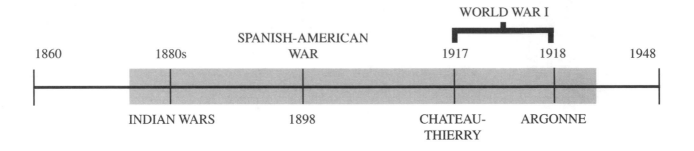

QUESTIONS FOR RESEARCH

1. Examine pictures of General Pershing. What is the character trait that seems most prominent? Why is it needed in the military service?

2. Sometimes Pershing's 10th Cavalry was called "buffalo soldiers." What service did those troops perform and why did they perform it?

3. Pershing's theories about rifle training and attack held up very well during the World War I battles of Chateau-Thierry, St. Mihiel, and Cantigny, but did not work as well in the largest American battle in World War I. Why?

NATIONAL STANDARDS CORRELATIONS

NCSS IId: (Time, Continuity, & Change) Identify and use processes important to reconstructing and reinterpreting the past, such as using a variety of sources, providing, validating, and weighing evidence for claims, checking credibility of sources, and searching for causality.
NSH Era 7, Standard 2: The changing role of the United States in world affairs through World War I

WEBSITES

http://www.americaslibrary.gov/jb/modern/jb_modern_pershing_1.html
"John J. Pershing Died July 15, 1948," The Library of Congress

http://www.nps.gov/prsf/history/bios/pershing.htm
"John 'Black Jack' Pershing (1860–1948)," National Park Service

http://www.army.mil/cmh-pg/books/AMH/AMH-18.htm
"World War I: The U.S. Army Overseas," The United States Army

Name: _____ Date: _____

John J. Pershing (cont.)

HISTORICAL FACTS

1. John Joseph Pershing was born in 1860, in _____, and spent his boyhood in _____, Missouri.

2. Pershing began a short teaching career at _____, but soon left that job to enter the _____.

3. He passed the examination for the _____, a school from which he graduated in 1886.

4. During the Spanish-American War, he was an officer with the 10th Cavalry, a unit of _____. Due to this and other associations with African-American troops, he was known throughout the service as "_____."

5. During the insurrection in the _____, Pershing campaigned against the fierce _____ tribesmen.

6. In 1906, because of an impression made upon _____, Pershing was promoted to the rank of brigadier general.

7. In 1916, he was placed in command of an army sent to capture the Mexican bandit _____.

8. In 1917, when the United States entered World War I, Pershing was given the command of the _____.

9. He was given the credit for the phrase "_____."

10. His insistence upon _____ and _____ tactics paid off.

11. He nurtured a bright young officer corps. Two of these men were _____ and _____.

12. Pershing demanded that _____ troops be maintained within the organization of the American Expeditionary Force.

101

Charles A. Lindbergh

1902–1974

When Charles Augustus Lindbergh died in 1974, there was a sudden remembrance of the deeds of this "last genuine American folk hero." Lindbergh was born in Michigan and raised in Little Falls, Minnesota. His father was a congressman from Minnesota for some time, and the Lindbergh family was strictly middle-class.

Lindbergh attempted college for two years, but his mediocre grades indicated his lack of interest in academic work. After taking a flying course in Lincoln, Nebraska, he made his first solo flight in an airplane he had bought for $500. Later commissioned as a lieutenant in the Missouri National Guard, he entered the Air Mail Service as a pilot between St. Louis and Chicago. Several times he barely survived crashes in Illinois cornfields.

By this time, he had become interested in a $25,000 prize offered by a hotel owner in New York for the first person to fly non-stop from New York to Paris. Lindbergh trained for the test by flying from San Diego to Long Island in 21 hours and 20 minutes.

Meanwhile, he had managed to interest the Ryan Airplane Company in his project. Since citizens of St. Louis raised the money for his new plane, Lindbergh called it the *Spirit of St. Louis*. The name could not have been more appropriate. He took off from Roosevelt Field, New York City, at 7:52 in the morning. He landed in Paris some 33 1/2 hours later.

He was now America's greatest hero. President Coolidge made him a colonel and sent a cruiser to bring him home. Lindbergh sold the story of his flight for a substantial sum, but this was, in a way, the beginning of a time of troubles. In 1932, the first child of his marriage to Anne Morrow Lindbergh was kidnapped and slain. Lindbergh was so distraught that he moved temporarily to France.

With the opening of war in Europe in 1939, Lindbergh took the unpopular stand of opposing America's entrance into the conflict. Even so, after Pearl Harbor, he volunteered for the service, but President F.D. Roosevelt, possibly out of spite, denied him a wartime command. But even as a civilian, he flew about fifty missions in the Pacific.

After the end of the war, Lindbergh retired into anonymity. Yet he managed to serve as a technical advisor to Pan American Airlines and helped in the establishment of the U.S. Air Force Academy. In 1974, finding that he had cancer, he went to Hawaii, determined to die in the place that he had learned to love the most. He refused all attempts to prolong his life and was buried, according to his wishes, by Hawaiian cowboys, in a place overlooking the Pacific Ocean.

The enormity of Lindbergh's success in flying from New York to Paris is best realized by observing the *Spirit of St. Louis*. Every available space in the plane was taken up with gasoline; the craft was, in essence, a flying bomb. In order to see, Lindbergh had to stick his head out of a side window for over 33 hours. Several times he barely missed death. He just managed to clear electric lines in his takeoff. Once during his flight, he fell asleep (He had been awake for over two days). He awoke just as his plane was over the surface of the ocean. He got lost over Ireland (he had almost no instrumentation), and even cut his motor to shout to an amazed Irish farmer.

Charles A. Lindbergh (cont.)

Still, he made it to Paris, the capital of the country in which Louis had become a saint. His great feat was just what a jaded world needed.

TIME LINE

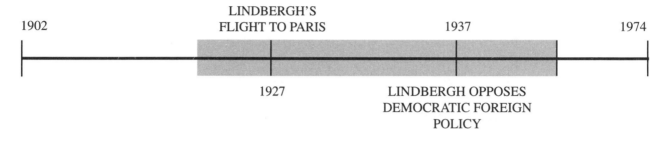

QUESTIONS FOR RESEARCH

1. The 1920s seem to have been a decade of hero worship for Americans. Will Rogers once said that every man who flew the Atlantic thereafter would be an imitation of Lindbergh. Name other American heroes of the twenties, and see if Rogers' remark fits them as well.

2. What was there about Lindbergh's personality and appearance that suited him for the role of all-American hero?

3. Lindbergh's attempts to keep the country out of war helped to destroy his reputation, but was he entirely wrong?

NATIONAL STANDARDS CORRELATIONS

NCSS IVf: (Power, Authority, & Governance) Explain conditions, actions, and motivations that contribute to conflict and cooperation within and among nations.
NSH Era 8, Standard 3: The causes and course of World War II, the character of the war at home and abroad, and its reshaping of the U.S. role in world affairs

WEBSITES

http://www.time.com/time/time100/heroes/profile/lindbergh01.html
"Charles Lindbergh," Time Inc.

http://historymatters.gmu.edu/d/5163/
"'An Independent Destiny for America': Charles A. Lindbergh on Isolationism," American Social History Productions, Inc.

http://lcweb2.loc.gov/ammem/today/jun11.html
"Today in History: Lindbergh Honored," The Library of Congress

Name: _____   Date: _____

Charles A. Lindbergh (cont.)

HISTORICAL FACTS

1. Lindbergh was born in _____ and raised in _____

   _____.

2. The Lindbergh family was strictly _____.

3. Lindbergh attended college for _____ years.

4. He was an Air Mail Service pilot between _____ and

   _____.

5. He became interested in a $25,000 prize for the first person to fly non-stop from

   _____ to _____.

6. He took off from Roosevelt Field, New York City, and landed in Paris _____

   hours later.

7. He was now America's greatest hero. _____ made him a

   colonel and sent a cruiser to bring him home.

8. In 1932, the first child of his marriage to Anne Morrow Lindbergh was _____

   and _____.

9. President Franklin Roosevelt denied him a command in World War II. But even as a civilian, he

   flew about _____ missions in the _____.

10. He helped in the establishment of the _____.

11. Every available space was taken up by gasoline in his plane, which was called _____

    _____, in flying from New York to Paris.

12. He got lost over _____, and he even cut his motor to shout to an amazed

    farmer.

104

Arthur Vandenberg

1884–1950

Arthur Vandenberg was a United States senator from Michigan. He was a Republican appointee to that body in 1928 and was re-elected in 1934. In the years following 1936, when war became a possibility in Europe, Vandenberg took the point of view most commonly called isolationist. That is: America should stay aloof from Europe's problems and should concentrate on her own. Any war in Europe, Vandenberg felt, should call for the strictest of isolationist policies on the part of the United States.

In general, President Franklin Roosevelt took the interventionist viewpoint. Many groups of Americans, especially in the eastern United States, thought that the United States should aid France, Britain, and Russia—after each of those nations had gone to war with Germany. Among the leading interventionists of the country were those associated with the Roosevelt administration, as well as many others in the literary and cultural world. Among the leading isolationists were Senators Robert Taft and Arthur Vandenberg, historian Charles Beard, Charles Lindbergh, and Herbert Hoover.

Even in retrospect, it is not easy to say that either side was totally wrong or totally right. The isolationists insisted that the United States was in no immediate danger of attack from Adolf Hitler (later documentation proved them correct). On the other hand, many intellectuals argued that America could not become a self-contained fortress (there is no present evidence to confirm or deny this argument).

In 1939, Adolf Hitler signed a pact with Russia that guaranteed Germany non-intervention by the Soviets if the German army invaded Poland. In the following September, Hitler sent his Panzer divisions roaring across the Polish border, and the Second World War was underway. France and Britain fulfilled their treaty with Poland by declaring war. Russia stayed out of it, and hoped to remain so, until Hitler turned upon that country and invaded.

In 1935, the United States issued a Proclamation of Neutrality, but slowly, President Roosevelt edged the nation towards war. By the fall of 1941, the U.S. and German navies were shooting at each other—hardly a state of peace—and American security patrols had advanced as far east as Iceland. This was months before Pearl Harbor.

In his relations with Japan, Roosevelt took an aggressive stance. He shut off shipments of oil, gas, and scrap iron, even though Japan had warned that it would get them from other areas if necessary. The other areas were such places as Indo-China (Vietnam), Java, Sumatra, etc. Late in 1941, President Roosevelt sent the fleet to Pearl Harbor and strongly suggested to the Japanese that they withdraw from portions of Indo-China and China. At this, the Japanese put into effect their previously drawn plans to attack Pearl Harbor on December 7, 1941.

With the attack upon Pearl Harbor, men such as Arthur Vandenberg became modified interventionists, cooperating with the administration at every turn. After all, the country was in a war for survival, and unity was necessary. Although Vandenberg was a candidate for the presidency several times, he was never

Arthur Vandenberg (cont.)

able to obtain the Republican nomination. In the end, he had to settle for the leadership of the Senate's foreign policy machinery. In 1950, he resigned because of a terminal illness, and the Senate lost one of its most able leaders.

TIME LINE

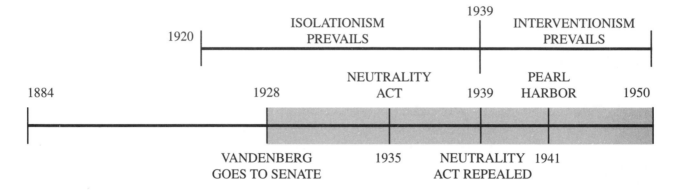

QUESTIONS FOR RESEARCH

1. Find instances of American destroyers engaged in action with German submarines before the United States entered the war. Who was the guilty party in these actions? Did Hitler want war with the United States in 1941?

2. In the 1960s, much of the intellectual community was against American intervention in Vietnam. In the 1930s, the situation seems to have been reversed. What were the attitudes of average Americans in the two time periods?

3. Research the German and Japanese views of American policy in 1941. Are they arguable?

NATIONAL STANDARDS CORRELATIONS

NCSS IIf: (Time, Continuity, & Change) Use knowledge of facts and concepts drawn from history, along with methods of historical inquiry, to inform decision-making about and action-taking on public issues.

NSH Era 8, Standard 3: The causes and course of World War II, the character of the war at home and abroad, and its reshaping of the U.S. role in world affairs

WEBSITES

http://www.navy.mil/navydata/ships/destroyers/greyhound.html
"The Destroyers: Greyhounds of the Sea," United States Navy

http://www.historyplace.com/unitedstates/vietnam/index-1969.html
"The Bitter End," The History Place

Name: _____   Date: _____

Arthur Vandenberg (cont.)

HISTORICAL FACTS

1. Arthur Vandenberg was a U.S. senator from _____.

2. When war became a possibility in Europe in 1936, Vandenberg took the point of view most commonly called _____.

3. In general, President Franklin Roosevelt took the _____ viewpoint.

4. Among the leading isolationists, including Vandenberg, were historian _____, _____, and _____.

5. The isolationists insisted that the United States was in no immediate danger of attack from _____.

6. In 1939, Adolf Hitler signed a pact with _____, which guaranteed Germany non-intervention if the German army invaded Poland.

7. _____ and _____ fulfilled their treaty with Poland by declaring war on Germany.

8. The United States, in 1935, issued a _____, but slowly President Roosevelt edged the nation towards war.

9. In his relations with _____, Roosevelt took an aggressive stance, shutting off shipments of oil, gas, and scrap iron.

10. Late in 1941, President Roosevelt sent the fleet to _____.

11. Pearl Harbor was attacked by the Japanese the morning of _____.

12. Although Vandenberg was a candidate for the presidency several times, he was never able to obtain the _____ nomination.

Douglas MacArthur

1880–1964

Douglas MacArthur was born in Little Rock, Arkansas. His father was General Arthur MacArthur, who joined the U.S. Army at the age of seventeen, and who won, during the course of his military career, numerous medals for heroism. Douglas MacArthur's mother was an extremely ambitious woman, who spent much time at West Point when young Douglas was a cadet in the U.S. Military Academy.

MacArthur graduated from the Academy in 1903 at the top of his class and immediately became a career officer in the army. He served in the Philippines, and on one occasion was engaged in a close gun battle with Filipino insurgents. From 1904 to 1914, MacArthur moved from post to post and, in 1916, was the engineering officer for General Pershing's campaign into Mexico.

When the United States entered World War I, MacArthur was given permission to organize national guard units into one grand unit known as the Rainbow Division—so named because it drew men from every state in the Union. A hard-fighting division, the Rainbow became known for its gallantry, as well as for the characteristics of its commander. MacArthur occasionally strolled about the battlefield under fire, wearing (as a general is entitled to do) odd variations of the uniform.

Following the war, MacArthur returned to the Philippines, where he commanded the Philippine division of the U.S. Army. In 1930, he became the Chief of Staff of the Army, a position he held until he was gently and subtly removed by President Franklin Roosevelt. In 1935, MacArthur became the major military advisor of the Philippine defense forces and attempted to prepare these troops for a possible war with Japan.

When conflict came in 1941, MacArthur was not as ready as he had supposed. His men were loosely trained, and the Japanese were able to destroy MacArthur's air force, even though the latter attacks took place days after Pearl Harbor. Japanese forces landing in the Philippines met little initial resistance, possibly because MacArthur was momentarily confused. He quickly recovered, however, and took his little army into the Bataan Peninsula, where his men fought on for several months, until overwhelmed by numerically superior Japanese forces.

By the time of the surrender of Bataan, MacArthur had been ordered to Australia by President Roosevelt. There he conducted two separate conflicts—the first against the Japanese, who were moving down the island chains of the Pacific, and the second against the Roosevelt administration, which tended to shortchange MacArthur on troops and supplies.

With an army consisting mostly of Australians in the beginning—Americans later—MacArthur moved the Japanese out of New Guinea. Then, with increasing numbers of American troops and ships, he moved into the Solomon and Admiralty Islands. Finally, MacArthur received enough national commitment to allow his "return" to the Philippines. In October 1944, American troops landed at Leyte. Almost a year later, MacArthur accepted the surrender of Japan on the USS *Missouri*.

MacArthur administered the military government in Japan for the next few years. In 1950, in response to the North Korean invasion of the Republic of South Korea, MacArthur led the U.N. forces in battle. After a personality clash with President Truman, MacArthur was removed from command.

MacArthur died in 1964. He is regarded by some—especially British military historians—as the most able Allied commander in World War II.

Douglas MacArthur (cont.)

TIME LINE

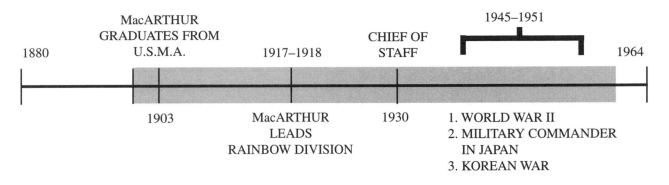

QUESTIONS FOR RESEARCH

1. What personality characteristics did MacArthur seem to have that caused some Americans to react adversely to him?

2. As indicated, MacArthur is sometimes regarded as the most brilliant commander in World War II. What strategy in World War II did MacArthur promote? What was the special achievement of MacArthur at the Inchon landing in Korea?

3. Both sides had their supporters in the Truman-MacArthur clash. What were the arguments propounded by the followers of both Truman and MacArthur?

NATIONAL STANDARDS CORRELATIONS

NCSS IVf: (Individual Development & Identity) Identify and describe the influence of perception, attitudes, values, and belief on personal identity.

NSH Era 8, Standard 3: The causes and course of World War II, the character of the war at home and abroad, and its reshaping of the U.S. role in world affairs

WEBSITES

http://www.trumanlibrary.org/whistlestop/study_collections/korea/large/sec4/kw163_1.htm
"Message from Commander in Chief United Nations Commander General Douglas MacArthur to the Joint Chiefs of Staff, dated 15 September 1950, pertaining to the landing at Inchon. Papers of Harry S Truman: Naval Aide Files," Harry S Truman Library and Museum/National Archives and Records Administration

http://www.loc.gov/exhibits/treasures/trm048.html
"Old Soldiers Never Die…," The Library of Congress

http://www.pbs.org/wgbh/amex/macarthur/
"MacArthur," Public Broadcasting Service/WGBH

Name: _____   Date: _____

Douglas MacArthur (cont.)

HISTORICAL FACTS

1. Douglas MacArthur was born in _____ in _____ .

2. Douglas was educated in the _____ .

3. MacArthur graduated from the academy in _____ , number _____ in his class, and immediately became a career officer in the army.

4. In 1916, MacArthur was the engineering officer for _____ in Mexico.

5. During World War I, MacArthur organized national guard units into one grand unit known as the

    _____ .

6. In 1930, he became the _____ of the army, a position he held until he was gently and subtly removed by _____ .

7. In 1935, MacArthur became the major military advisor of the _____

    _____ .

8. Japanese forces landing in the Philippines met little resistance until _____ where MacArthur fought on for several months—until finally overwhelmed by numerically superior Japanese forces.

9. By the time of the surrender of Bataan, MacArthur had been ordered to _____ by President Roosevelt.

10. MacArthur moved the Japanese out of _____ , and the

    _____ and _____ Islands.

11. Finally, MacArthur received enough national commitment to allow his "return" to the

    _____ .

12. MacArthur accepted the surrender of Japan on the USS *Missouri* in _____ .

Ronald Reagan

1911–2004

Ronald Reagan was the fortieth president of the United States. After the turbulent times of the 1960s and 1970s and the low morale following the Vietnam War, the Reagan presidency was seen as a time when national pride was restored and economic recovery began.

Ronald Reagan

Reagan grew up in Dixon, Illinois. He worked summers as a lifeguard to earn money for college. He was credited with saving 77 lives in six years. He received a degree from Eureka College in Illinois in 1932. After graduating, he became a sportscaster in Des Moines, Iowa.

In 1937, while in California to cover baseball spring training, he did a screen test for Warner Brothers and was soon appearing in motion pictures. During World War II, he enlisted in the army and made training and morale-boosting films. He rose to the rank of captain.

Reagan's marriage to actress Jane Wyman ended in divorce in 1948 after they had two children, one of whom was adopted. In 1952, he married Nancy Davis, who was also an actress. They had two children as well.

After serving 12 terms as the president of the Screen Actors Guild, Reagan decided to run for governor of California in 1966. He won the election and served two terms as governor. He was able to cut the state's debt and learned to work with the legislature and to use television as a method of gaining public support. This helped earn his reputation as "the Great Communicator."

Reagan campaigned for the Republican nomination for president in 1968 and 1976 but was unsuccessful. In 1980, he won the nomination and chose one of his competitors, George H.W. Bush, as his vice president. The Reagan-Bush team easily defeated the incumbent president Jimmy Carter in the general election, winning by 8.3 million popular votes and 489–49 in the electoral college. When he was reelected in 1984, defeating former Vice President Walter Mondale, the margin was even greater.

Early in his presidency on March 30, 1981, Reagan was shot by a mentally ill man in an assassination attempt. He was hospitalized for several weeks but made a full recovery. Three others were also wounded in the attack.

One of Reagan's top priorities as president was to improve the economy. Inflation and unemployment were high. In August 1981, he signed the Economic Recovery Act, which included the largest tax cut in U.S. history. Reagan's approach to economics came to be known as "Reaganomics." He would reduce taxes to encourage savings, investment, and business expansion. He felt that less government involvement would stimulate the creation of more small businesses and more jobs. In 1982, the nation experienced a severe recession and unemployment reached 12 million. However, by 1984, inflation and unemployment had been brought under control.

Reagan also pushed Congress to spend more money to strengthen the military. He saw the Soviet Union as an "evil empire" and pledged to help any nation that was struggling against Communism. The United States supported rebels in Afghanistan who were fighting the Soviet-backed government, and it supported Iraq in its war with Iran. Reagan ordered the bombing of Libyan cities when it was suspected the country's leader, Muammar Qadaffi, was financing terrorist groups. In 1983, U.S. troops were sent to the Caribbean nation of Granada when Communist rebels overthrew the government and threatened to kidnap Americans on the island.

The "Iran-Contra Affair" became a scandal during the Reagan presidency. White House officials arranged for arms and supplies to be sold to Iran at a low price, and then, in turn, have Iran send aid to the Contras in Nicaragua. The Contras were fighting the pro-Communist government in Nicaragua, but Congress had voted against sending them any direct aid. When hearings were held to investigate this policy, it was never determined if Reagan knew what his aides were doing or not.

Perhaps Reagan's greatest foreign policy success was in his dealings with the Soviet Union. He

Ronald Reagan (cont.)

began by beefing up the military and setting up missiles in West Germany that could reach Soviet targets in five minutes. However, when the new Soviet Premier Mikhail Gorbachev began changes in the Soviet Union that would eventually lead to democracy, Reagan saw the changes as good for peace. He attended meetings in Switzerland and Iceland with the Soviet leader. Agreements were made to destroy many of the missiles on both sides. In June 1987, Reagan visited West Berlin and demanded, "Mr. Gorbachev, tear down this wall!" By November 1989, the Berlin Wall had fallen and the Cold War was over.

The Reagans left the White House in January 1989 and retired to Bel Air, California. In 1994, Reagan announced that he had Alzheimer's disease. He remained out of the public eye, cared for by his wife Nancy. Ronald Reagan died on June 5, 2004.

In 2005, the Discovery Channel ran a television series called *The Greatest American,* in which viewers were asked to choose who, in all of American history, was "The Greatest American." After narrowing the field of 100 down to 25 and then five, the people chose Ronald Reagan as "The Greatest American."

TIME LINE

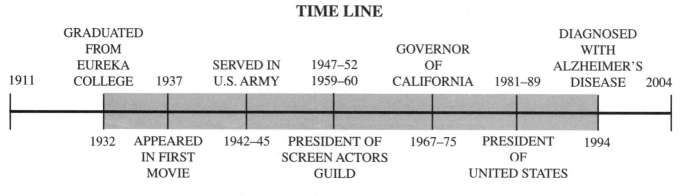

QUESTIONS FOR RESEARCH

1. Ronald Reagan was not always a Republican. Research his early political beliefs and why he became a Republican.
2. What jobs had Reagan held that taught him how to be "the Great Communicator," as he was often called? Watch one of his movies.
3. Research Alzheimer's Disease. What are the symptoms? What is being done to find a cure?

NATIONAL STANDARDS CORRELATIONS

NCSS VIi: (Power, Authority, & Governance) Give examples and explain how governments attempt to achieve their stated ideals at home and abroad.

NSH Era 10, Standard 1: Recent developments in foreign policy and domestic policies

WEBSITES

http://www.whitehouse.gov/history/presidents/rr40.html
"Ronald Reagan," The White House

http://www.alzheimers.org/pubs/adfact.html
"Alzheimer's Disease Fact Sheet," Alzheimer's Disease Education & Referral Center

http://www.reagan.utexas.edu/
"Archives: Ronald Reagan Presidential Library," National Archives and Records Administration

Name: _____   Date: _____

Ronald Reagan (cont.)

HISTORICAL FACTS

1. Ronald Reagan grew up in Dixon, Illinois, and worked as a _____ in the sum-

    mers to earn money for college.

2. Reagan's first job after college was as a _____.

3. After doing a screen test for Warner Brothers in 1937, he was soon appearing in _____

    _____.

4. Reagan rose to the rank of _____ in the U.S. army during World War II.

5. _____ was Reagan's first wife. They were divorced in 1948.

6. Reagan served as _____ of the Screen Actors Guild.

7. Reagan married _____ in 1952.

8. He served two terms as _____ of California.

9. One of Reagan's nicknames was "the _____ _____."

10. Ronald Reagan and George H.W. Bush defeated _____ and Walter

    Mondale in the election of 1980.

11. Improving the _____ was a top priority for the Reagan administration.

12. Reagan made several agreements with the Soviet Union when Soviet Premier _____

    _____ began to make changes in the government that would lead to democracy.

13. In 1994, Reagan announced that he had _____ disease and remained out of the

    public eye until his death in 2004.

14. In 2005, Ronald Reagan was named "The _____ _____."

Name: _____   Date: _____

U.S. History Outline Map

Directions: Use this map to label locations associated with specific people profiled in this book.

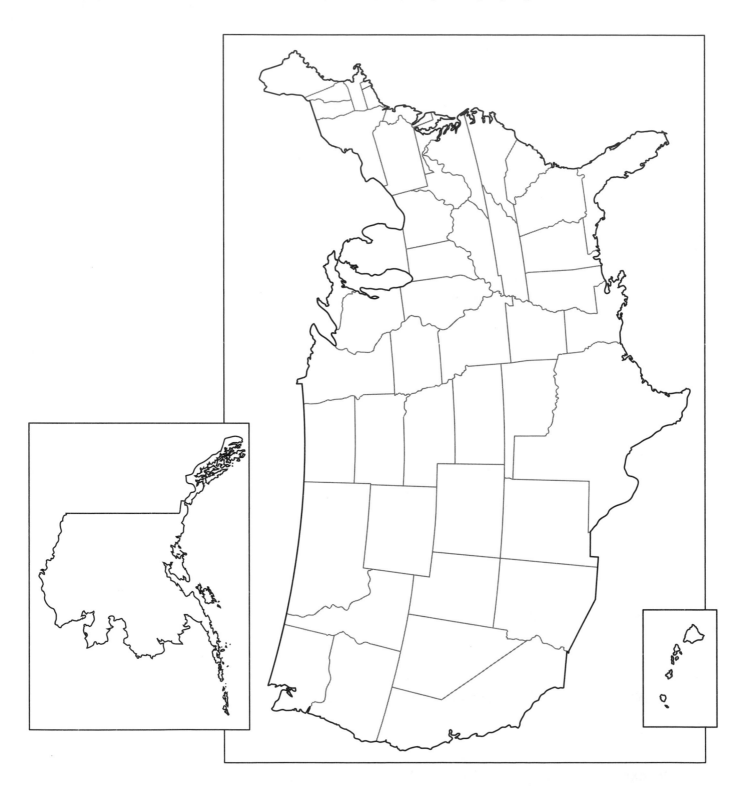

Bibliography/Further Reading

Adams, J. T. *Album of American History* *

Adams, J. T. *Atlas of American History*

Amacher, Richard. *Benjamin Franklin*

The American Heritage Picture History of the Civil War

Anderson, Nels. *Desert Saints: The Mormon Frontier in Utah*

Andrews, Avery. *My Friend and Classmate: John J. Pershing*

Brockunier, Samuel H. *The Irrepressible Democrat: Roger Williams*

Bates, E. S. *American Faith: Its Religious, Political, and Economic Foundations*

Beach, Seth. *Daughters of the Puritans*

Benson, Michael. *Ronald Reagan* (Presidential Leaders)

Bowen, Catherine Drinker. *Yankee From Olympus*

Brodie, F. M. *No Man Knows My History: The Life of Joseph Smith, the Mormon Prophet*

Brown, R. C. *The Human Side of American History*

Buckmaster, H. *Women Who Shaped History*

Carey, John. *Joseph Warren: Physician, Politician, Patriot*

Cather, Willa. *O Pioneers!* (a novel)

Catton, Bruce. *Grant Moves South*

Cleaves, Freeman. *Rock of Chickamauga*

Collins, A. C. *The Story of America in Pictures*

Crane, Verner W. *Benjamin Franklin and a Rising People*

Curti, M. *The Growth of American Thought*

Davis, Kenneth. *The Hero: Charles A. Lindbergh and the American Dream*

Dictionary of American Biography

Drucker, P. *Indians of the Northwest Coast*

D'Souza, Dinesh. *Ronald Reagan: How an Ordinary Man Became an Extraordinary Leader*

Eggleston, Edward, and Seelye, Lillie. *Tecumseh and the Shawnee Prophet*

Elliot, Charles W. *Winfield Scott: The Soldier and the Man*

Filler, L. *The Crusade Against Slavery*

Ford, H. J. *Washington and His Colleagues: Chronicles of America, Vol. 14*

Franklin, John H. *Reconstruction* **

Bibliography/Further Reading (cont.)

Fredricks, Edgar J. *MacArthur: His Mission and Meaning*

Fuess, C. *Carl Schurz*

Gabriel, R. H., ed. *The Pageant of America: A Pictorial History of the United States*

Gerson, Noel B. *Rebel! A Biography of Tom Paine*

Graham, Shirley. *Booker T. Washington: Educator of Hand, Head, and Heart*

Harvey, Rowland H. *Samuel Gompers, Champion of the Toiling Masses*

Henderson, Archibald. *The Campus of the First State University*

Hofstader, Richard. *The Age of Reform; From Bryan to F.D.R.*

Jellison, Charles A. *Ethan Allen: Frontier Rebel*

Johnson, Darv. *The Reagan Years* (World History Series)

Journal of Negro History, Vol. VII, 1922

Knox, D. W. *A History of the United States Navy*

Lilienthal, David. *TVA: Democracy on the March*

Lowie, R. *Indians of the Plains*

Lowitt, Richard. *George Norris: The Making of a Progressive*

Marshall, Helen E. *Dorothea Dix, Forgotten Samaritan*

Meigs, C. *As the Crow Flies (a novel)*

Meigs, C. *The Violent Men*

Millis, Walter. *The Martial Spirit*

Morison, S. E., ed. *The Development of Harvard University Since the Inauguration of President Eliot*

Palmer, Frederick. *John J. Pershing: General of the Armies*

Powderly, T. V. *The Path I Trod: The Autobiography of Terence V. Powderly*

Powderly, T. V. *Thirty Years of Labor, 1859–1889*

Quaife, Milo. *Autobiography of Black Hawk* (annotated ed.)

Rankin, Hugh F. *Francis Marion: The Swamp Fox*

Reagan, Ronald. *An American Life: The Autobiography*

Ross, Walter S. *The Last Hero: Charles A. Lindbergh*

Shaw, A. H. *Story of a Pioneer*

Sheer, G. and Rankin, H. *Rebels and Redcoats*

Bibliography/Further Reading (cont.)

Sickels, E. M. *In Calico and Crinoline—True Stories of American Women, 1608–1865*

Singletary, O. A. *The Mexican War*

Slosson, E. F. *Great American Universities*

Slosson, P. W. *The Great Crusade and After (Chapter 5)*

Spencer, Samuel R. *Booker T. Washington and the Negro's Place in American Life*

Stanton, Elizabeth Cady. *Eighty Years and More*

Stevens, Frank E. *The Black Hawk War*

Sullivan, M. *Our Times*

Thorne, Florence. *Samuel Gompers: American Statesman*

Tucker, Glenn. *Tecumseh: Vision of Glory*

Tudor, William. *The Life of James Otis of Massachusetts*

Vandenberg, A., ed. *The Private Papers of Senator Vandenberg*

Ware, N. J. *The Labor Movement in the United States, 1860–1895*

Willoughby, Charles and Chamberlain, John. *MacArthur, 1941–1951*

Winslow, Ola E. *Master Roger Williams, A Biography*

Woodward, William E. *Tom Paine: America's Godfather, 1737–1809*

Zucker, Norman L. *George W. Norris: Gentle Knight of American Democracy*

(*__Note:__ There are no recent biographies of Benjamin Lundy, but the *Dictionary of American Biography* does list various readings applicable to his story.)

(**__Note:__ To understand Blanche Bruce, it is necessary to understand the policy of Reconstruction.)

Historical Facts Answer Keys

Roger Williams (p. 8)
1. London, England
2. Cambridge University
3. minister
4. Boston, 1631
5. Yes
6. separation
7. Narragansett tribe
8. land title for Rhode Island
9. England, charter
10. separation of church and state, and religious freedom
11. Anne Hutchinson
12. King Philip's War

Benjamin Franklin (p. 11)
1. Boston
2. 16
3. self-taught
4. printer
5. Silence Dogood
6. Philadelphia
7. *Poor Richard's Almanack*
8. improved mail service, special messenger service between cities, world's first subscription library, etc.
9. famous kite experiments with lightning and electricity
10. Declaration of Independence
11. France
12. abolition of slavery

James Otis (p. 14)
1. West Barnstable, Massachusetts
2. Harvard College
3. lawyer
4. British Writs of Assistance
5. customs officers
6. colonial merchants
7. Stamp Act
8. Townshend Acts
9. Massachusetts colonial government

10. rescind
11. British revenue officers
12. insane
13. killed, lightning
14. taxes

Joseph Warren (p. 17)
1. Roxbury, Massachusetts
2. Harvard College, Boston physician
3. physicians
4. Stamp Act
5. president of the Provincial Assembly
6. Massachusetts colonial militia
7. American Revolution
8. Breed's Hill, Boston Harbor
9. 50
10. 1,000
11. sharpshooters
12. Bunker Hill

Ethan Allen (p. 20)
1. Litchfield, Connecticut
2. New York, New Hampshire
3. Green Mountain Boys
4. 100 pounds
5. Fort Ticonderoga
6. Boston
7. Montreal
8. Vermont
9. Vermont militia
10. British, traitorous
11. farming, revolution
12. publications

Thomas Paine (p. 23)

1. no
2. England
3. no, 13 years
4. Benjamin Franklin
5. Revolutionary War
6. *Common Sense*
7. British Empire
8. Washington's Army
9. Pennsylvania, New York
10. *Rights of Man*
11. *Age of Reason*
12. New York, England

Francis Marion (p. 26)

1. guerilla fighter
2. Thomas Sutter, Andrew Pickens, and Elijah Clark
3. Swamp Fox
4. 44
5. South Carolina Provincial Congress
6. sprained ankle, South Carolina
7. surprise attacks, quick withdrawals
8. supply wagons
9. lead
10. three rounds
11. Pee Dee River, Snow Island
12. South Carolina legislature

John Jay (p. 29)

1. statesman, diplomat
2. private tutors, King's College
3. Robert R. Livingston
4. Spain
5. West
6. Alexander Hamilton, James Madison
7. *The Federalist*
8. New York
9. Supreme Court
10. neutrality
11. out of war
12. to his 800-acre farm

Tecumseh (p. 32)

1. Ohio, 1768
2. long knives
3. father and brother
4. unity
5. Tenskwatawa, Shawnee Prophet
6. eclipse of the sun
7. British
8. oratorical
9. William Henry Harrison
10. the Prophet, Tippecanoe Creek
11. Brigadier general, British
12. Richard Johnson

Zebulon Pike (p. 35)

1. 33
2. 15
3. Thomas Jefferson, Louisiana
4. Mississippi River
5. southwest
6. Osage, Arkansas
7. Pike's
8. Spanish
9. St. Louis
10. northern Mexico, Mexican War
11. 1812, general
12. York, killed

Black Hawk (p. 38)

1. Lorado Taft
2. Black Hawk, Rock River
3. French, Spanish
4. William Henry Harrison
5. treaties
6. long knives
7. Tecumseh
8. Americans
9. Illinois, Mississippi
10. settlement
11. Black Hawk
12. Jackson, Chief Keokuk

Dolley Madison (p. 41)
1. Guilford County, North Carolina
2. John Todd, Jr.
3. James Madison
4. Revolutionary period
5. *The Federalist Papers*
6. secretary of state
7. Great Britain
8. Washington, D.C.
9. George Washington
10. social affairs
11. president's house
12. ice cream

Benjamin Lundy (p. 44)
1. Sussex County, New Jersey
2. saddler's
3. anti-slavery society
4. *The Genius of Universal Emancipation*
5. Baltimore
6. recolonization
7. Haiti
8. William Lloyd Garrison
9. *The Genius*
10. Philadelphia
11. *The War in Texas*
12. Lowell, Illinois

Winfield Scott (p. 47)
1. 50
2. War of 1812, Mexican War, Civil War
3. William and Mary
4. 1812
5. Queenston Heights, British
6. 6, 300
7. brigadier general
8. Lundy's Lane
9. manual of arms, infantry tactics
10. Mexico
11. Franklin Pierce
12. Union

David Glasgow Farragut (p. 50)
1. Knoxville, Tennessee
2. captain
3. Civil War, Vicksburg
4. Confederacy, Confederate
5. lashed, *Hartford*
6. "Damn the torpedoes! Four bells!"
7. Confederate, Union
8. General Hood
9. E.R.S. Canby
10. Farragut and David D. Porter, Union
11. full admiral
12. in the hard school of reality

Brigham Young (p. 53)
1. second president
2. Joseph Smith
3. Vermont
4. *The Book of Mormon*
5. Kirtland, Ohio
6. Twelve Apostles
7. three
8. Great Salt Lake
9. insects
10. gold rush
11. massacred
12. evangelical work

Dorothea Lynde Dix (p. 56)
1. Hampden, Maine; Massachusetts
2. tuberculosis
3. school for young girls
4. East Cambridge House of Corrections, insane
5. three-year investigation
6. 300 jails, 500 almshouses, 18 state prisons
7. *A Memorial to the Legislature of Massachusetts*
8. mentally insane
9. asylums
10. England
11. Union
12. 85

George Thomas (p. 59)

1. George Thomas
2. southern
3. Virginia
4. General Rosecrans, Tennessee
5. Chattanooga
6. Chickamauga, Thomas's
7. Chattanooga
8. U.S. Grant
9. W.T. Sherman
10. Missionary Ridge
11. General Hood
12. Grant, Sherman, Sheridan

Philip Henry Sheridan (p. 62)

1. County Cavan
2. United States Military Academy
3. Civil War
4. brigadier general
5. Rosecrans'
6. Chickamauga
7. Missionary Ridge
8. U.S. Grant
9. Shenandoah Valley
10. Lee
11. major general, Division of the Gulf
12. Reconstruction period, hostile Native American tribes

Helen Hunt Jackson (p. 65)

1. Amherst, Massachusetts; 1830
2. silver, gold, Dakotas, Colorado, and Nevada
3. Union Pacific, Central Pacific
4. Native American tribes
5. 275,000
6. Sioux, Crow, Blackfeet; Cheyenne, Kiowa, Apache; Ute, Snake, Bannock
7. scarcity of troops
8. 450, Cheyenne, Arapaho
9. Colonel Custer's
10. buffalo, disease, whiskey
11. *A Century of Dishonor*
12. special commissioner

Blanche K. Bruce (p. 68)

1. Virginia
2. Missouri
3. co-racial
4. plantation
5. politician
6. United States Senate
7. civil rights
8. Amnesty
9. federal aid
10. flood, navigation
11. Reconstruction
12. appointed

Justin Smith Morrill (p. 71)

1. Vermont
2. store clerk
3. 38
4. Congress
5. Republican
6. six
7. 32
8. Ways and Means
9. Land-Grant
10. vetoed
11. 1862
12. 30,000
13. land-grant
14. Agriculture

Elizabeth Cady Stanton (p. 74)

1. Victorian
2. Emma Willard, law
3. temperance
4. obey
5. Lucretia Coffin Mott
6. Mrs. Stanton
7. women's suffrage
8. Susan B. Anthony
9. divorce, suffrage, professional life
10. National American Woman Suffrage
11. seven
12. *History of Woman Suffrage*

Carl Schurz (p. 77)
1. Prussia
2. kindergarten
3. Lincoln's
4. brigadier general
5. St. Louis
6. Joseph Pulitzer
7. Liberal Republican Party
8. Horace Greeley
9. Rutherford B. Hayes
10. secretary of the interior
11. civil service
12. New York *Evening Post*

Alfred Thayer Mahan (p. 80)
1. West Point, New York
2. United States Naval Academy
3. *Congress*
4. Civil War
5. *The Gulf and Inland Waters*
6. War College
7. *The Influence of Sea Power Upon History, 1660–1763*
8. 1890
9. navy
10. colonies, colonies
11. empire
12. Japanese

Booker T. Washington (p. 83)
1. northern philanthropists
2. Hampton Institute, Tuskegee Institute
3. Booker Taliaferro Washington
4. Hampton Institute, bricklayer
5. Malden, West Virginia
6. Alabama
7. Tuskegee
8. vocational
9. National Association for the Advancement of Colored People
10. spokesman
11. Theodore Roosevelt's
12. stone, loaf of bread

Terence Powderly (p. 86)
1. 1860
2. industrialization, immigration
3. protection
4. machinist
5. Union
6. the Knights of Labor
7. Philadelphia
8. unskilled
9. Grand or General Master Workman
10. Scranton, Pennsylvania
11. strikes
12. Chicago
13. American Federation of Labor

Samuel Gompers (p. 89)
1. London, 1850
2. 13
3. Cigarmakers' International Union
4. sweat, spit
5. tuberculosis
6. American Federation of Labor
7. 265,000
8. 4.1
9. neither
10. anti-strike, strike
11. women, children
12. 1924, A.F.L.-C.I.O.

Charles William Eliot (p. 92)
1. educational
2. Harvard College
3. professor
4. president
5. graduate
6. women
7. *Reports of the President of Harvard College*
8. *Harvard Classics*
9. fifteen
10. homes
11. 1850, 1930
12. the world of learning
13. 92

Oliver Wendell Holmes, Jr. (p. 95)

1. March 8, 1841
2. 21
3. poet, physician
4. Civil War
5. three
6. Harvard Law
7. *American Law Review*, *The Common Law*
8. Chief Justice
9. Supreme Court
10. Chief Justice
11. justice, honor
12. of the great legal minds

George W. Norris (p. 98)

1. 1861
2. statesmen
3. independence
4. Valparaiso University
5. U.S. House of Representatives
6. Progressive
7. United States Senator
8. League of Nations
9. utilities
10. Muscle Shoals
11. $5 million
12. Tennessee Valley Authority
13. 30
14. Twentieth
15. fascism

John J. Pershing (p. 101)

1. Linn County, Missouri; Laclede
2. an African-American school, Kirksville Normal School
3. U.S. Military Academy
4. African-American soldiers, "Black Jack"
5. Philippines, Moro
6. President Theodore Roosevelt
7. Pancho Villa
8. American Expeditionary Forces
9. "Lafayette, we are here."
10. rifle, attack
11. George Catlett Marshall, Douglas Mac-Arthur
12. American

Charles A. Lindbergh (p. 104)

1. Michigan; Little Falls, Minnesota
2. middle-class
3. Two
4. St. Louis, Chicago
5. New York, Paris
6. 33 1/2
7. President Coolidge
8. kidnapped, slain
9. 50, Pacific
10. Air Force Academy
11. *The Spirit of St. Louis*
12. Ireland

Arthur Vandenberg (p. 107)

1. Michigan
2. isolationist
3. interventionist
4. Charles Beard, Charles Lindbergh, Herbert Hoover
5. Adolf Hitler
6. Russia
7. France, Britain
8. Proclamation of Neutrality
9. Japan
10. Pearl Harbor
11. December 7, 1941
12. Republican

Douglas MacArthur (p. 111)

1. Little Rock, Arkansas; 1880
2. U.S. Military Academy
3. 1903, one
4. General Pershing
5. Rainbow Division
6. Chief of Staff, President Franklin Roosevelt
7. Philippine Defense Forces
8. Bataan
9. Australia
10. New Guinea, Solomon, Admiralty
11. Philippines
12. 1945

Ronald Reagan (p. 113)

1. lifeguard
2. sportscaster
3. motion pictures
4. captain
5. Jane Wyman
6. president
7. Nancy Davis
8. governor
9. Great Communicator
10. Jimmy Carter
11. economy
12. Mikhail Gorbachev
13. Alzheimer's
14. Greatest American